ZODIAC KILLER: THE INTERVIEWS

ZODIAC KILLER: THE INTERVIEWS

Volume 3

ALAN R. WARREN
MICHAEL BUTTERFIELD

Copyright

Zodiac Killer: The Interviews
Written by Alan R. Warren
Published by House of Mystery

Copyright @ 2020 by Alan R. Warren

All rights reserved. No part of this book may be reproduced, scanned, or distributed in any printed or electronic form without permission of the author. The unauthorized reproduction of a copyrighted work is illegal. Criminal copyright infringement, including infringement without monetary gain, is investigated by the FBI and is punishable by fines and federal imprisonment. Please do not participate in or encourage privacy of copyrighted materials in violation of the author's rights. Purchase only authorized editions. This is a work of nonfiction. No names have been changed, no characters invented, no events fabricated.

Cover design, formatting, layout, and editing by Evening Sky Publishing Services

Published in United States of America
ISBN (Paperback): 978-1-989980-24-8
ISBN (eBook): 978-1-989980-23-1

CONTENTS

Foreword · vii
Introduction · xvi
The Zodiac Murders · xxi
The Zodiac Communications · xxxvii

1. **Ciphers And Cryptograms** · 1
   Interview with David Oranchak
2. **Don Cheney** · 18
   Interview with Drew Hurst Beeson
3. **Joseph James DeAngelo Jr.** · 40
   Interview with Anne Penn
4. **Earl Van Best Jr** · 56
   Interview with Gary L. Stewart
5. **Unabomber** · 78
   Interview with Dr. Mark G. Hewitt
6. **George Hodel | The Black Dahlia Killer** · 115
   Interview with Steve Hodel
7. **Edward Wayne Edwards** · 126
   Interview with John A. Cameron
8. **Michael O'Hare** · 149
   Interview with Ray Grant
9. **Zodiac Hoax** · 170
   Interview with Thomas Horan

The Zodiac 340 Cipher: Mystery Solved	205
About Alan R. Warren	223
About Michael Butterfield	225
Also in the House of Mystery Radio Show Interview Series	227

Foreword

BY MICHAEL BUTTERFIELD

The man who called himself "the Zodiac" remains one of the most terrifying and elusive villains in true crime history. He bragged about his murders in the first letters sent to newspapers along with a coded message he claimed would reveal his identity. More than half a century later, the case is still unsolved, and the killer has escaped justice, leaving the mystery clouded by speculation, misinformation, and falsehoods.

Law enforcement investigators continue the search for suspects while amateur sleuths routinely claim that they have identified the Zodiac. Some of these individuals are just attention-seekers, but others are true believers convinced they have solved the case. Such claims are rarely supported by any credible evidence linking a specific suspect to the crimes.

According to some estimates, more than 2,500 suspects have been investigated over the years, including the so-called "prime suspect," a convicted child molester named Arthur Leigh Allen. Former *San Francisco Chronicle* cartoonist Robert Graysmith referred to Allen using the pseudonym "Bob Hall Starr" in his best-selling book *Zodiac*. Graysmith's version of the Zodiac story was largely fictionalized, and his attempts to convince readers of Allen's guilt blurred the lines between fact and fiction. Much of the evidence said to implicate Allen in the Zodiac crimes later proved to be distorted, exaggerated, and even invented. Allen continues to be a popular suspect, but the public's opinion about his possible guilt is often based on the fictional version of the evidence rather than the facts.

Unlike Allen, the majority of the men referred to as "suspects" have never been considered actual suspects by law enforcement. Instead, these men were known as suspects simply because at least one person accused them. The accusers were retired police officers, writers, amateur detectives, and others disappointed when they were dismissed or ignored by investigators. As a result, these theorists rely on the media to spread their claims, in the form of books, websites, and YouTube videos. Many people only hear about the Zodiac case in the context of these accusations, and the names of the accused are repeated despite the lack of credible evidence linking them to the Zodiac crimes.

Gary Stewart claimed his father was the Zodiac, and his book, *The Most Dangerous Animal of All,* was followed by a documentary series of the same name, which dismantled his theories. In 1987, Gareth Penn published his book *Times 17* and claimed former Harvard lecturer Michael O'Hare was the Zodiac. Later, Ray Grant claimed that Penn and O'Hare worked together to commit the crimes, with the help of their parents, as part of some elaborate project. Penn and Grant relied heavily on their interpretations of the Zodiac's communications, but both failed to provide actual evidence to support their accusations.

John Cameron claimed that a man named Edward Wayne Edwards was responsible for the Zodiac murders and many other infamous crimes. Still, his theories were based mainly on personal speculation and assumptions instead of actual evidence. Anne Penn claimed that the "Golden State Killer" Joseph James DeAngelo was also the Zodiac, but offered no evidence to establish any real connection between the two cases. Steve Hodel claimed that his father was responsible for the Zodiac attacks, the gruesome murder of Elizabeth Short, a.k.a. "The Black Dahlia," and other crimes. Hodel's case against his father was based on speculation and theories about geometry and the crimes scenes' geographic locations. Hodel's factual errors about the Zodiac case were compounded by his geometric and geographic errors, and he failed to establish any link between his father and the Zodiac. Mark Hewitt published a book including the reasons behind his conclusion that Ted Kaczynski, a.k.a. "the Unabomber," was also the Zodiac. His theory was based mostly on his opinions regarding perceived similarities between the two killers and his interpretations of the Zodiac's communications compared to the Unabomber's writings and Kaczynski's personality.

Theories linking the Zodiac to other notorious crimes may seem appealing because these scenarios resemble the familiar fictional world where villains are larger than life caricatures of human evil. Some theorists are rejected by law enforcement and then claim that investigators are part of an official cover-up or some conspiracy to protect a suspect or conceal the real motives behind the Zodiac murders. Conspiracy theories are popular in film and fiction, and sinister plots are often blamed for the lack of resolutions in many unsolved mysteries. The belief that unknown forces operating in the shadows have somehow obstructed justice may seem like a more comforting explanation than the cold reality that one man committed a series of horrific murders and sent taunting letters to newspapers but was never caught. For similar reasons, some people believe the claims that the Zodiac never actually existed, that the crimes were unrelated and that the letters were part of a hoax created by reporters, members of law enforcement, or others. Such theories may be entertaining but are not supported by or compatible with the known facts. After he stabbed a couple at Lake Berryessa, the killer walked from the scene of the crime and stopped to write a message on the victims' car door. The bootprints found at the scene showed the killer's path, and the handwriting on the door was similar to the writing of the Zodiac letters. At least one questioned document examiner concluded that the same person was responsible for the letters and the message on the victim's car. The myriad bizarre scenarios required also rendered the hoax theory problematic at best.

One useful exercise provides a valuable perspective when examining and assessing the men referred to as "suspects." One can write down the names of 10 known suspects, but then we can immediately discard 9 of those names because, barring some conspiracy involving multiple suspects, we know that only one of those men could be the Zodiac. One can write down the names of ten of the people who have accused suspects, and we can immediately conclude that at least 9 of them are wrong about the Zodiac's identity. Absent any credible evidence linking any of the named suspects to the Zodiac crimes, a more likely explanation indicates that all 10 of the accusers were wrong.

Any effort to positively identify the Zodiac will rely on the available evidence, including handwriting, fingerprints, palm prints, DNA, and more. San Francisco police believed the killer left a fingerprint at the scene of the last known Zodiac murder. Still, its quality may be insufficient to produce a positive match when compared to a suspect's fingerprints. Other possible Zodiac fingerprints were found on some of the letters, and a palm print was found on a suspected Zodiac letter sent in 1974. Handwriting comparisons may link a suspect to the Zodiac messages, but investigators need to find other evidence to build a case for conviction. At least three Zodiac messages were accompanied by a piece of a victim's bloodstained shirt, and this evidence established a link between the letter-writer and the crimes. The letters were either written by the killer or someone involved in the crimes, before or after. They also had access to the victim's clothing taken from the scene of a crime.

Estimates of the Zodiac's age at the time of the attacks indicate that he may be in his late 70s or 80s if he is still alive today. If the Zodiac is dead, he may never be identified without discovering physical evidence linking a specific individual to the crimes. The best hope to solve the case may be modern advances in DNA technology and forensic genealogy. In 2018, a search of DNA ancestry databases helped identify DNA found at the scene of a crime attributed to the Golden State Killer in 1980. The authorities were able to arrest Joseph James DeAngelo, a former police officer in his early 70s. The search for DNA in the Zodiac case includes an examination of the envelopes and stamps used by the killer. A complete genetic profile obtained from saliva on the envelopes or stamps could be used to identify a suspect if one or more of his relatives add their familial DNA to one of the ancestry databases which shares that information with law enforcement agencies.

An unconventional avenue of investigation has produced actual results. In December 2020, one of the Zodiac's unsolved ciphers was finally cracked by computer programmers Jarl Van Eycke, Sam Blake, and David Oranchak. By working together on the internet from three different countries, the trio discovered the killer's encryption method and unlocked the message which had been hidden for 51 years. Their remarkable achievement creates hope that more answers may be found. One cipher, accompanied by the teasing promise, "My name is," leads many to believe that the solution could solve the case. Until then, the debate about various theories and suspects continues, and the identity of the Zodiac remains a mystery.

Michael Butterfield

December 2020

Introduction

The *House of Mystery Radio Show* has been on the air for ten years now, broadcasting in over a dozen cities in the United States, including KKNW 1150 A.M. Seattle/Tacoma, KCAA 106.5 F.M. Los Angeles/102.3 F.M. Riverside/1050 A.M. Palm Springs. I started the show to find out as much information on the world's mysteries in areas of Crime, Science, Religion, history, paranormal, and more. Like most people, I have heard stories, rumors, and read books or watched documentaries on television, but would seldom hear one direct answer to a question.

Throughout my time recording interviews, I sought out people who had themselves

INTRODUCTION   xvii

researched a subject enough to have written a book or created a documentary, or even people involved in the event or topic that would have first-hand knowledge.

In most cases, the strange thing was that there was a popular or mainstream idea about what happened, one reported at the time of the event, but then there was an alternative idea. Most writers who had books or shows that did well quite often disagreed with the current theory and would accuse the media of faking the story and hiding the truth from everyone.

An example would be "Who shot JFK?" There has been a well-known theory reported by different government agencies and news media that most people in America have come to accept as the truth. But since the original Warren Report on JFK's assassination, there have been hundreds of theories promoted by many authors and lots of research completed.

In this series, we review the most accepted explanation on the topic. Then, we follow up with each of the alternative theories presented during our interviews with the person or people reporting them. There will be no committed answer at the end of the book. Our goal is to provide a concise review of the extraordinary things we learned during the show's interviews.

Each book in this series lays out the topic's details and then follows up with what we've learned from each guest. This book, like the others in the House of Mystery Radio Show Interviews Series, does not attempt to solve the case but only review it. It is an excellent reference for researchers and a good overview for people who don't know the topic well. Similar to the other volumes in this series, only the highlights of each interview will be included.

All of these interviews, and more, are available to listen to on my website: *alanrwarren.com/hom-zodiac-killer-interviews*

Volume 3 of the Interview Series, "Zodiac Killer," covers another serial killer who has stayed in the spotlight for years after their case has gone cold. It's been over 40 years now, and fascination with the Zodiac is still going strong. I asked most authors of this case why they thought it was still so popular, and the most common answer I received was the fact that it was an unsolved case. Like Jack the Ripper, we have many suspects and numerous clues, but not much hard evidence.

The Zodiac case has several great researchers to ask for help from during our investigation and interviews period, and it's not always easy to pick someone. Michael Butterfield was an excellent choice for us, as he explained things well, with logic, and in a way that was easy to understand. With his 20 plus years of experience on the Zodiac case, choosing him made sense. Butterfield has sat in almost all of the Zodiac guest interviews over the last five years and has contributed his own Zodiac update segments as well.

Michael Butterfield (zodiackillerfacts.com) is a writer who has conducted extensive research on the Zodiac case since the 1990s. As a recognized leading expert on the unsolved crime, he has served as a media source and consultant for news articles, documentaries, the History Channel series *The Hunt for the Zodiac Killer*, and Director David Fincher's major motion picture *Zodiac*. Butterfield has also consulted on the following:

the Zodiac documentary *Case Reopened*, the History Channel series *Mystery Quest*, the E! Canada series *The Shocking Truth*, the Reelz Channel documentary *The Real Story of Zodiac*, the HLN series *Very Scary People*, the documentary produced for Japanese television *Darkside Mystery*, and the podcast series *Monster: The Zodiac Killer*. He is also the producer of the podcast series *Zodiac: A to Z*. He is a contributing author for *True Crime: Case Files*, *True Crime Magazine*, and the two-volume collection of essays titled *A History of Evil in Pop Culture*.

Over the last ten years, I have heard from people who believe the Zodiac Killer was a relative of theirs, and I've also heard the theory that he was an already well-known convicted serial killer. Some authors offer suggestions for new or already considered suspects. There is also an author who argues the Zodiac Killer didn't even exist and that Zodiac was a hoax.

Another part of this case discussed and debated a great deal by researchers is the letters and ciphers from the killer. Like Jack the Ripper case, there are many that question if some or all of the letters are valid.

The Zodiac Murders

Like with the Jack the Ripper mystery, there are victims who everyone agrees was committed by the serial killer, but there are victims who are questioned as well. After the primary layout of the agreed-upon murders, I will list the other murder victims.

The "Zodiac Killer" is the pseudonym of an American serial killer who operated in Northern California from the late 1960s to the early 1970s. His identity remains unknown. The Zodiac murdered five known victims in Benicia, Vallejo, Napa County, and San Francisco between December 1968 and October 1969. He targeted young couples, with two of the men surviving attempted murder. He also murdered a male cab driver. The Zodiac himself once claimed to have murdered 37 victims in letters to the newspapers; however, investigators agree on only seven confirmed victims, two of whom survived.

Agreed Upon Murders

David Arthur Faraday, 17, and **Betty Lou Jensen**, 16, were shot and killed on December 20, 1968, on Lake Herman Road, within Benicia's city limits. These first murders of the high school students are widely thought to be committed by the Zodiac Killer.

On their first date, the couple planned to attend a Christmas concert at Hogan High School about three blocks from Jensen's home. Instead, the couple visited a friend before stopping at a local restaurant and then driving out on Lake Herman Road. At about 10:15 p.m., Faraday parked his mother's Rambler in a gravel turnout, a well-known lovers' lane. Shortly after 11:00 p.m., their bodies were found by Stella Borges, who lived nearby. The Solano County Sheriff's Department investigated the crime, but no leads developed. Robert Graysmith, a political cartoonist who became intensely interested in solving the Zodiac case and later authored the book *Zodiac*, believed another car pulled into the turnout just before 11:00 p.m. and parked beside the couple. The killer then exited his vehicle and walked toward the Rambler, possibly ordering the couple to get out. Jensen appeared to have exited the car first, yet when Faraday was halfway out, the killer shot him in the head. Then, he shot Jensen five times in the back as she fled. Her body was found 28 feet from the car.

Michael Renault Mageau, 19, and **Darlene Elizabeth Ferrin**, 22, were shot on July 4, 1969, in the parking lot of Blue Rock Springs Park in Vallejo. While Mageau survived the attack despite being shot in the face, neck, and chest, Ferrin was pronounced dead on arrival at Kaiser Foundation Hospital. Mageau described his attacker as a 26 to 30-year-old white male, 195 to 200-pounds or possibly more, 5-foot 8-inches tall, with short, light brown curly hair.

Just before midnight on July 4, 1969, Darlene Ferrin and Michael Mageau drove into the Blue Rock Springs Park in Vallejo, about four miles from the Lake Herman Road murder site, and parked. While the couple sat in Ferrin's car, another car drove into the lot and parked alongside them but almost immediately drove away. Returning about 10 minutes later, the car parked behind them. The driver then exited the vehicle and approached the passenger side door, carrying a flashlight and a 9 mm gun. The killer directed the flashlight into Mageau's and Ferrin's eyes before shooting at them, firing five times. Both victims were hit, and several bullets passed through Mageau and into Ferrin. The killer walked away from the car, but upon hearing Mageau's moaning, he returned and shot each victim twice more before driving off.

On July 5, 1969, at 12:40 a.m., a man phoned the Vallejo Police Department to report and claim responsibility for the attack. The caller also took credit for the murders of Jensen and Faraday six-and-a-half months earlier. Police traced the call to a phone booth at a gas station at Springs Road and Tuolumne, located less than a mile from Ferrin's home and only a few blocks from the Vallejo Police Department.

Bryan Calvin Hartnell, 20, and **Cecelia Ann Shepard**, 22, were stabbed on September 27, 1969, at Lake Berryessa in Napa County. Hartnell survived eight stab wounds to the back, but Shepard died two days later as a result of her injuries.

On September 27, 1969, Pacific Union College students Bryan Hartnell and Cecelia Shepard were picnicking at Lake Berryessa on a small island connected by a sand spit to Twin Oak Ridge. A white man, about 5-foot 11-inches tall, weighing more than 170 pounds, with combed greasy brown hair approached them wearing a black executioner-type hood with clip-on sunglasses over the eyeholes and a bib-like device on his chest that had a white three-by-three-inch cross-circle symbol on it.

He approached them with a gun, which Hartnell believed to be a .45. The hooded man claimed to be an escaped convict from a jail with a two-word name, in either Colorado or Montana, where he had killed a guard and subsequently stolen a car. He explained that he now needed their car and money to go to Mexico, as the vehicle he had been driving was "too hot." He had brought precut lengths of plastic clothesline and told Shepard to tie up Hartnell. The killer checked and tightened Hartnell's bonds after discovering Shepard had bound his hands loosely. Hartnell initially believed this event to be a bizarre robbery, but the man drew a knife and stabbed them both repeatedly, Hartnell suffering six and Shepard ten wounds in the process.

The killer then hiked 500 yards back up to Knoxville Road, drew the cross-circle symbol on Hartnell's car door with a black felt-tip pen, and wrote beneath it, "Vallejo/12-20-68/7-4-69/Sept 27–69–6:30/by knife."

At 7:40 p.m., the killer called the Napa County Sheriff's office from a payphone to report his latest crime. The caller first stated to the operator that he wished to "report a murder, no, a double murder," before saying he had committed the crime. The phone was found, still off the hook, minutes later at the Napa Car Wash on Main Street by KVON radio reporter Pat Stanley. It was only a few blocks from the sheriff's office, yet 27 miles from the crime scene. Detectives were able to lift a still-wet palm print from the telephone but could never match it to any suspect.

After hearing their screams for help, a man and his son fishing in a nearby cove discovered the victims and summoned help by contacting park rangers. Napa County Sheriff's deputies Dave Collins and Ray Land were the first law enforcement officers to arrive at the crime scene. Cecelia Shepard was still conscious when Collins arrived, providing him with a detailed description of the attacker. Hartnell and Shepard were taken to Queen of the Valley Hospital in Napa by ambulance. Shepard lapsed into a coma during transport to the hospital and never regained consciousness. She died two days later, but Hartnell survived to recount his tale to the press.

Paul Stine, 29, was shot and killed on October 11, 1969, in the Presidio Heights neighborhood in San Francisco, two weeks after the Hartnell-Sheppard attack. A white male passenger entered a cab, driven by Paul Stine, at the intersection of Mason and Geary Streets, a block from Union Square. He asked to be taken to Washington and Maple Streets in Presidio Heights. For reasons unknown, Stine drove one block past Maple to Cherry Street, and the passenger then shot Stine once in the head with a 9 mm, took Stine's wallet and car keys, and tore away a section of Stine's bloodstained shirttail. This passenger was seen by three teenagers across the street at 9:55 p.m., who called the police while the crime was in progress. They saw the man wiping the cab down before walking away towards the Presidio, one block to the north.

Two blocks from the crime scene, patrol officer Don Fouke and Eric Zelms, responding to the call, observed a white man walking along the sidewalk east on Jackson Street and stepping onto a stairway leading up to the front yard of one of the homes on the north side of the street. Fouke estimated the white male pedestrian to be 35 to 45-years old, 5-foot 10-inches tall, with a crew cut. The description was similar to but slightly older than the one given by the teenagers who saw the killer in and out of Stine's cab. They said it was a 25 to 30-year-old white male with a crewcut about 5-foot 8-inches to 5-foot 9-inches tall. Unfortunately, the police radio dispatcher initially alerted officers to be on the lookout for a black suspect, so Fouke and Zelms drove past him without stopping to check him out. A search ensued, but no suspects were found.

The Stine murder was initially thought to be a routine robbery that had escalated. However, on October 13th, the *San Francisco Chronicle* received a letter from Zodiac containing a piece of Stine's bloody shirt and taking credit for the killing. The three teen witnesses worked with a police artist to prepare a composite sketch of Stine's killer. A few days later, this police artist returned, working with the witnesses to prepare a second composite sketch of the killer. Detectives Bill Armstrong and Dave Toschi were then assigned to the case. The San Francisco Police Department investigated an estimated 2,500 suspects over a period of years.[1]

Possible Murder Victims

There have been other murders attributed to the Zodiac Killer, but not all researchers or people involved in the case agree with these being included:

Robert Domingos, 18, and **Linda Edwards**, 17, were shot and killed on June 4, 1963, on a beach near Gaviota. There are some similarities between their attack and the Zodiac's attack at Lake Berryessa six years later.

On June 4, 1963, high school senior Robert Domingos and fiancée Linda Edwards were shot dead on a beach near Lompoc, having skipped school that day for "Senior Ditch Day." Police believed the assailant attempted to bind the victims, but when they freed themselves and attempted to flee, the killer shot them repeatedly in the back and chest with a .22 caliber weapon. The killer placed their bodies in a small shack and then tried, unsuccessfully, to burn the structure to the ground.

In a *Vallejo Times-Herald* story appearing on November 13, 1972, Bill Baker of the Santa Barbara County Sheriff's Office postulated that the 1963 murders of a young couple in Northern Santa Barbara County might have been the work of the Zodiac Killer.

Cheri Jo Bates, 18, was stabbed to death and nearly decapitated on October 30, 1966, at Riverside City College in Riverside. Bates's possible connection to the Zodiac only appeared four years after her murder when *San Francisco Chronicle* reporter, Paul Avery, received a tip regarding similarities between the Zodiac killings and the circumstances surrounding Bates's death.

On October 30, 1966, Cheri Jo Bates, a student at Riverside Community College, spent the evening at the campus library annex until it closed at 9:00 p.m. Neighbors reported hearing a scream around 10:30 p.m. Bates was found dead the next morning, a short distance from the library, between two abandoned houses slated to be demolished for campus renovations. She was brutally beaten and stabbed to death.

The wires in her Volkswagen's distributor cap had been pulled out. A man's Timex watch with a torn wristband was found nearby. The watch had stopped at 12:24 a.m., but police believe the attack occurred much earlier.

A month later, on November 29, 1966, nearly identical typewritten letters were mailed to the Riverside police and the *Riverside Press-Enterprise*, titled "The Confession." The author claimed responsibility for the Bates murder, providing details of the crime not released to the public. The author warned that Bates "is not the first, and she will not be the last."

In December 1966, a poem was discovered carved into the bottom side of a desktop in the Riverside City College library called "Sick of living/unwilling to die." The poem's language and handwriting resembled that of the Zodiac's letters. It was signed with what was assumed to be the initials "R.H." During the 1970 investigation, Sherwood Morrill, California's top "Questioned Documents" examiner, expressed his opinion that the Zodiac wrote the poem.

On April 30, 1967, exactly six months after the Bates murder, Cheri's father Joseph, the *Press-Enterprise*, and the Riverside police all received nearly identical letters in a handwritten scrawl. The *Press-Enterprise* and police copies read, "Bates had to die there will be more," with a small scribble at the bottom that resembled the letter "Z." Joseph Bates' copy read, "She had to die there will be more;" this time without the "Z" signature.

On March 13, 1971, five months after Avery's article linking the Zodiac to the Riverside murder, the Zodiac mailed a letter to the *Los Angeles Times*. In the letter, he credited the police, instead of Avery, for discovering his "Riverside activity. But they are only finding the easy ones. There are a hell of a lot more down there."

The connection between Cheri Jo Bates, Riverside, and the Zodiac Killer remains uncertain. Paul Avery and the Riverside Police Department maintained that the Zodiac did not commit the Bates homicide. They did agree that some of the Bates letters may have been his work to claim credit for it, albeit falsely.

Donna Lass, 25, was last seen September 6, 1970, in Stateline, Nevada. Lass was a nurse at the Sahara Tahoe Hotel and Casino. She worked until about 2:00 a.m. on September 6, 1970, treating her last patient at 1:40 a.m. Later that day, Lass's employer and landlord received phone calls from an unknown male falsely saying that Lass had left town due to a family emergency. Donna Lass was never heard from again. What appeared to be a gravesite was discovered near the Clair Tappan Lodge in Norden, California, on Sierra Club property. But an excavation yielded only a pair of sunglasses.

On March 22, 1971, a postcard to the Chronicle, addressed to Paul Avery and believed to be from the Zodiac, appeared to claim responsibility for the disappearance of Donna Lass on September 6, 1970. Fabricated from advertisements and magazine lettering, the postcard featured a scene from Forest Pines Condominiums. It included the text phrases, "Sierra Club," "Sought Victim 12," "peek through the pines," "pass Lake Tahoe areas," and "around in the snow." Zodiac's cross circle symbol was in both the usual return address spot and the lower right section of the postcard's front face.

Kathleen Johns, 22, was allegedly abducted on the night of March 22, 1970. That night, Johns was driving from San Bernardino to Petaluma to visit her mother. She was seven months pregnant and had her 10-month-old daughter beside her. While heading west on Highway 132, near Modesto, a car behind her began honking its horn and flashing its headlights. She pulled off the road and stopped. The man in the car stopped as well and parked behind her. He approached her car, claiming he observed that her right rear wheel was wobbling, and offered to tighten the lug nuts for her. After finishing his work, the man drove off.

When Johns pulled forward to re-enter the highway, the wheel almost immediately came off the car. The man returned, offering to drive her to the nearest gas station for help. She and her daughter climbed into his car. During the ride, the car passed several service stations, but the man did not stop. For about 90 minutes, he drove back and forth around the backroads near Tracy. When Johns asked why he was not stopping, he would change the subject. When the driver finally stopped at an intersection, Johns jumped out with her daughter and hid in a field. The driver searched for her with his flashlight telling her he would not hurt her before eventually giving up. Unable to find her, he got back into his car and drove off. Johns hitched a ride to the police station in Patterson.

When Johns gave her statement to the Sergeant on duty, she noticed the police composite sketch of Paul Stine's killer and recognized him as the man who had abducted her and her child. Fearing he might come back and kill them all, the Sergeant had Johns wait, in the dark, at the nearby Mil's Restaurant. When her car was found, it had been gutted and torched. Most accounts say he threatened to kill her and her daughter while driving them around, but at least one police report contradicted that. Johns's account to Paul Avery of the *Chronicle* indicated her abductor left his car and searched for her in the dark with a flashlight; however, she stated he did not leave the vehicle in one report she made to the police.

---

1. Zodiac Killer — Wikipedia. https://en.wikipedia.org/wiki/340_cypher

The Zodiac Communications

Usually, murderers and criminals try to hide from law enforcement. The Zodiac was different. He had no problem sending off letters to the press and police to let them know he was there. And he taunted them as much as he could.

In addition to letters, he sent cryptograms that allegedly contained secret information about the killer's identity. All they had to do was crack the code behind the cipher to discover who he was. This boldness was something both the newspapers and the police had not dealt with before. They wondered how to respond. When the Zodiac demanded his letters be published, they questioned if they should do it or not. The problem was that the police didn't realize that by publishing the letters and cryptograms, they allowed the public to be part of the investigation and play Zodiac's game.

The detectives scoured the letters and ciphers for clues, and the public got in on the action too. Everyone wanted to crack the hidden codes and be the one to discover the identity of the Zodiac Killer.

Another problem law enforcement faced was figuring out if all the letters received were indeed from the Zodiac and not some person trying to garner public attention.

Below I have listed the communications by Zodiac, in order of date, assigned names, and primary contents in the letters:

Z408 Cipher Dated July 31, 1969

The first cipher from the Zodiac received on July 31, 1969, was his longest at 408 characters. The killer split the message into three pieces of equal length and mailed two to newspapers in San

Francisco, the *San Francisco Chronicle* and the *San Francisco Examiner,* and the other to a newspaper in nearby Vallejo, the *Vallejo Times-Herald.*

The nearly identical letters took credit for the shootings at Lake Herman Road and Blue Rock Springs. Each letter included one-third of a 408-symbol cryptogram, which the killer claimed contained his identity. The killer demanded that they be published, or he would go on a killing rampage.

On August 1, 1969, the three letters prepared by the Zodiac were published. An article printed alongside the code in the *Chronicle* quoted Vallejo Police Chief Jack E. Stiltz as saying, "We're not satisfied that the letter was written by the murderer," and requested the writer send a second letter with more facts to prove his identity.

About a week later, on August 8, 1969, schoolteacher Donald Harden and his wife Bettye of North Salinas, California, contacted the *San*

Francisco Chronicle with their solution. They cracked the 408-symbol cryptogram.

Bettye guessed that the message would begin with the word "I." She also believed the word "KILL," or "KILLING," or even the phrase "I LIKE KILLING," would appear somewhere in the message. It contained a misspelled message in which the killer seemed to reference the film, *The Most Dangerous Game*.

He also said he was collecting slaves for the afterlife. No name appears in the decoded text, and the killer said he would not give away his identity because it would slow down or stop his slave collection.[1]

THE ZODIAC COMMUNICATIONS

PAGE 1

```
I LIKE KILLING PEOPLE
BECAUSE IT IS SO MUCH
FUN IT I(S) MORE FUN THAN
KILLING WILD GAME I(N) THE
FORREST BECAU
SE MAN IS THE MOST DAN
GEROUS ANAMAL OF ALL
TO KILL SOMETHING G(IVES)
```

A was found to mean A and S. 5 errors

| Z408 Part 1 sent to the *Vallejo Times-Herald*

PAGE II

Z408 Part 2 sent to the *San Francisco Examiner*

Z408 Part 3 sent to the *San Francisco Chronicle*

xliv   THE ZODIAC COMMUNICATIONS

Envelope Cover to Z408

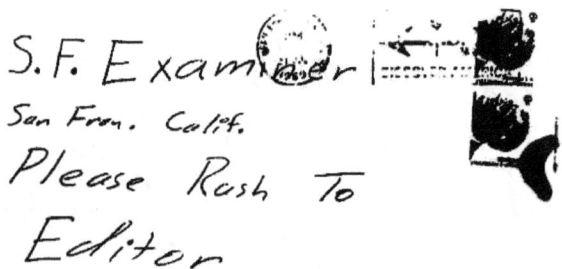

Envelope Cover to Z408

Envelope Cover to Z408

The Debut of Zodiac Letter Dated August 7, 1969

On August 7, 1969, another letter was received at the *San Francisco Examiner* with the salutation *"Dear Editor, This is the Zodiac speaking."* This letter was the first time the killer used this name, Zodiac, for identification. The letter was a response to Chief Stiltz's request for more detail that would prove he had killed Faraday, Jensen, and Ferrin. In the letter, Zodiac included details about the murders that had not yet been released to the public and a message to the police that they would have him when they cracked his code.

Dear Editor
This is the Zodiac speaking.
In answer to your asking for
more details about the good
times I have had in Vallejo,
I shall be very happy to
supply even more material.
By the way, are the police
haveing a good time with the
code? If not, tell them to cheer
up; when they do crack it
they will have me.
On the 4th of July
I did not open the car door, The
window was rolled down allready.
The boy was originaly sitting in
the front seat when I began
fireing. When I fired the first
shot at his head, he leaped
backwords at the same time
thus spoiling my aim. He ended
up on the back seat then
the floor in back thashing about
very violently with his legs;
thats how I shot him in the

The Debut of Zodiac Letter Pg. 1

tacks. I did leave the scene
of the killing with squealling
tires + racing engine as described
in the Vallejo paper. I drove away
quite slowly so as not to draw
attention to my car.
The man who told the police
that my car was brown was a
negro about 40-45 rather shabbly
dressed. I was at this phone
booth haveing some fun with the
Vallejo cop when he was walking
by. When I hung the phone up
the damn X @ thing began to
ring & that drew his attention
to me + my car.
Last Christmass
In that epasode the police were
wondering as to how I could
shoot + hit my victoms in the
dark. They did not openly state
this, but implied this by saying
it was a well lit night + I could
see the silowets on the horizon.
Bullshit that area is surounded

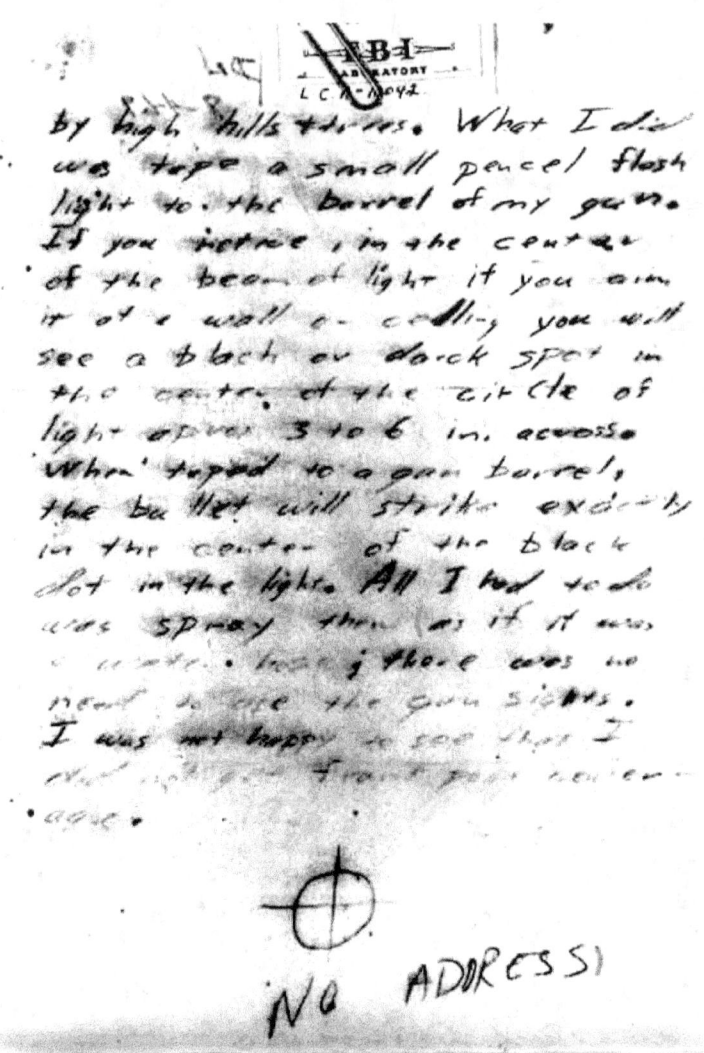

The Debut of Zodiac Letter Pg. 3

The Stine Letter Dated October 13, 1969

The Zodiac Killer took responsibility for Stine's death in "The Stine Letter," postmarked October

13, 1969. With the letter, he enclosed a piece of the victim's bloodied shirt. His messages also often included a crosshairs symbol, which resembled a rifle's sight, the same symbol on the hood worn during his September 1969 attack.

> This is the Zodiac speaking. I am the murderer of the taxi driver over by Washington St & Maple St last night, to prove this here is a blood stained piece of his shirt. I am the same man who did in the people in the north bay area.
> The S.F. Police could have caught me last night if they had searched the park properly instead of holding road races with their motor cicles seeing who could make the most noise. The car drivers should have just parked their cars & sat there quietly waiting for me to come out of cover.
> School children make nice targets, I think I shall wipe out a school bus some morning. Just shoot out the front tire & then pick off the kiddies as they come bouncing out.

1 THE ZODIAC COMMUNICATIONS

Z340 Cipher Dated November 8, 1969

On November 8, 1969, the Zodiac mailed the "340 Cipher," comprised of 63 characters, and the "Dripping Pen Card" to the *San Francisco Chronicle*. This cipher was finally solved in December 2020 by computer programmers Jarl Van Eycke, Sam Blake, and David Oranchak of *ZodiacKillerCiphers.com*.

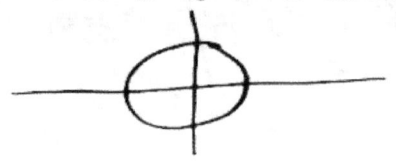

THE ZODIAC COMMUNICATIONS li

The Dripping Pen Card Dated November 8, 1969

Sorry I haven't written,

but I just washed my pen...

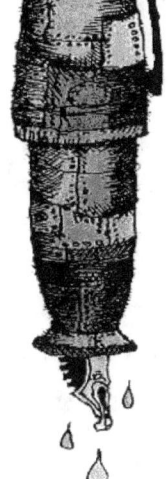

The Bus Bomb Letter Dated November 6, 1969

2/6

This is the Zodiac speaking up to the end of Oct I have killed 7 people. I have grown rather angry with the police for their telling lies about me. So I shall change the way the collecting of slaves. I shall no longer announce to anyone. when I comitt my murders, they shall look like routine robberies, killings of anger, + a few fake accidents, etc.

The police shall never catch me, because I have been too clever for them.

1 I look like the description passed out only when I do my thing, the rest of the time I look entirly different. I shall not tell you what my descise consists of when I kill

2 As of yet I have left no fingerpoints behind me contrary to what the police say

> The Bus Bomb Letter Pg. 1 sent to the *San Francisco Chronicle*

2/6

in my killings I wear trans-
parent finger-tip guards. All it
is is 2 coats of airplane cement
coated on my finger tips — quite
unnoticible & very efective.
3 my killing tools have been bought
en through the mail order out-
fits before the ban went into
efect. except one & it was
bought out of the state.
So as you see the police don't
have much to work on. If you
wonder why I was wipeing the
cab down I was leaving fake clews
for the police to run all over town
with, as one might say, I gave
the cops som bussy work to do to
keep them happy. I enjoy needling
the blue pigs. Hey blue pig I
was in the park — you were useing
fire trucks to mask the sound
of your cruzeing prowl cars. The
dogs never come with in 2
blocks of me + they were to
the west + there was only 2

The Bus Bomb Letter Pg. 2 sent to the *San Francisco Chronicle*

groaps of parking about 10 min
apart then the motor cicles
went by about 150 ft away
going from south to north west.
ps. 2 cops pulled a goof abot 3
min after I left the cab. I was
walking down the hill to the
park when this cop car pulled up
+ one of them called me over
+ asked if I saw any one
acting sapicisous or strange
in the last 5 to 10 min + I said
yes there was this man who
was running by waveing a gun
+ the cops peeled rubber +
went around the conner as
I directed them & I dissap-
eared into the park a block +
a half away never to be seen
again.
"Hey pig doesnt it rile you up
to have you noze rubed in your
booboos?
If you cops think I'm going to take
on a bus the way I stated I was,
you deserve to have holes in your
heads.

> The Bus Bomb Letter Pg. 3 sent to the
> *San Francisco Chronicle*

Take one bag of ammonium nitrate fertlizer + 1gal of stove oil + damp a few bags of gravel on top + then set the shit off + will positivily ventalate any thing that should be in the way of the Blast.
The death machiene is allready made. I would have sent you pictures but you would be nasty enough to trace them back to developer + then to me, so I shall descuibe my masterpiece to you. The nice part of it is all the parts can be boughs on the open market with no questions asked.
1 bat. pow clock — will run for aprox 1 year
1 photo electric switch
2 copper leaf springs
2 6V ca- bat
1 flash light bulb + reflector
1 mirror
2 18" cardboard tubes black with shoe polish inside + outs

The Bus Bomb Letter Pg. 4 sent to the *San Francisco Chronicle*

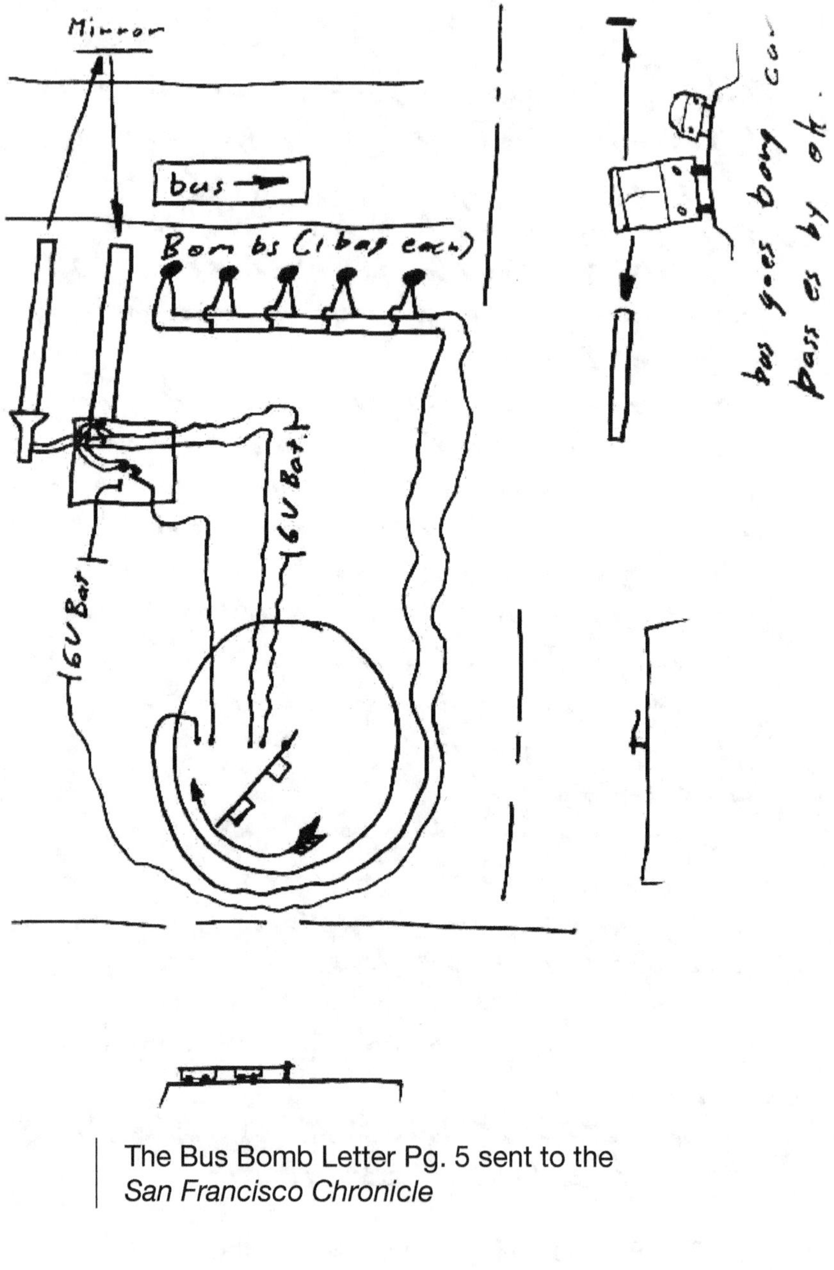

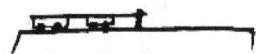

The Bus Bomb Letter Pg. 5 sent to the *San Francisco Chronicle*

the system checks out from one end to the other in my tests. What you do not know is whether the death machine is at the sight or whether it is being stored in my basement for future use. I think you do not have the man power to stop this one by continually searching the road sides looking for this thing. + it wont do to re roat + re schedule the busses bec ause the bomb can be adapted to new conditions.
Have fun!! By the way it could be rather messy if you try to bluff me.

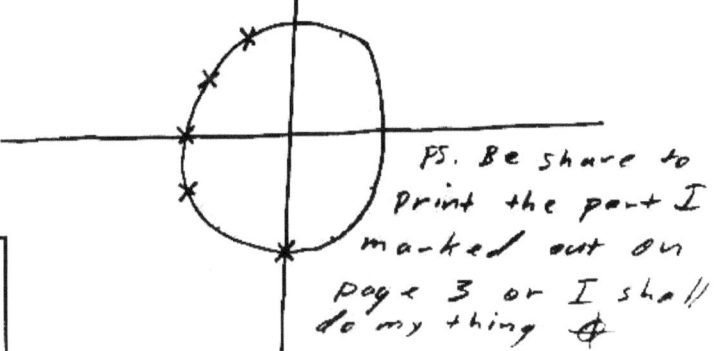

PS. Be shure to print the part I marked out on page 3 or I shall do my thing ⊕

The Bus Bomb Letter Pg. 6 sent to the *San Francisco Chronicle*

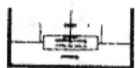

To prove that I am the Zodiac, Ask the Vallejo cop about my electric gun sight which I used to start my collecting of slaves.

The Bus Bomb Letter Pg. 7 sent to the *San Francisco Chronicle*

The Melvin Belli Letter Dated December 20, 1969

Dear Melvin

This is the Zodiac speaking I wish you a happy Christmass. The one thing I ask of you is this, please help me. I cannot reach out for help because of this thing in me wont let me. I am finding it extreamly dificult to hold it in check I am afraid I will loose control again and take my nineth & posibly tenth victom. Please help me I am drownding. At the moment the children are safe from the bomb because it is so massive to dig in & the triger mech requires much work to get it adjusted just right. But if I hold back too long from no nine I will loose ~~complet~~ all controol of my self & set the bomb up. Please help me I can not remain in control for much longer.

Z1313 Cipher | My Name Is Letter Dated April 20, 1970

On the surface, the killer's shortest cipher appeared to be the most important. It is preceded by the words "My name is ———." Would the killer indeed reveal his name?

> This is the Zodiac speaking
> By the way have you cracked the last cipher I sent you?
> My name is ———
>
> A E N ✚ ⊗ K ⊗ M ⊙ ⌡ N A M
>
> I am mildly cerous as to how much money you have on my head now. I hope you do not think that I was the one who wiped out that blue meannie with a bomb at the cop station. Even though I talked about killing school children with one. It just wouldnt doo to move in on someone elses toritory. But there is more glory in killing a cop then a cid because a cop can shoot back. I have killed ten people to date. It would have been a lot more except that my bas bomb was a dud. I was swamped out by the rain we had a while back.

| My Name Is Letter/Z13 Pg. 1

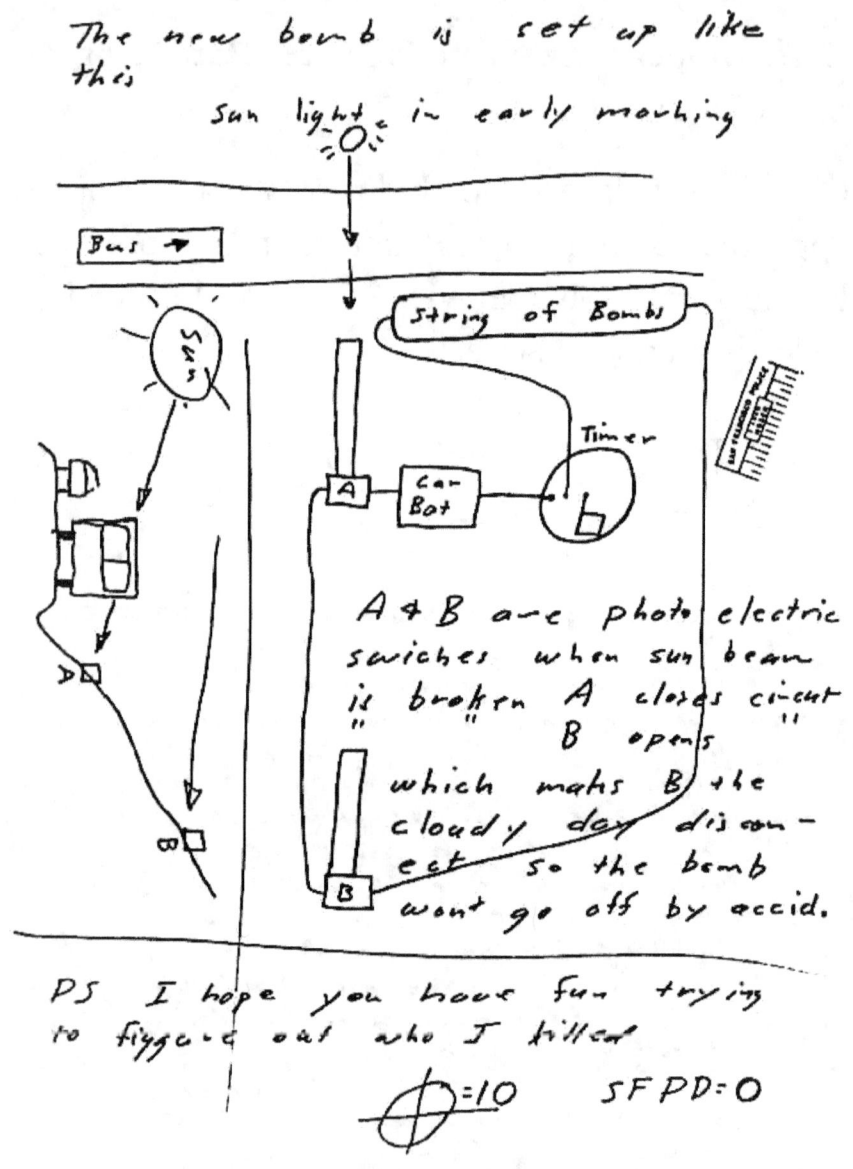

My Name Is Letter/Z13 Pg. 2

THE ZODIAC COMMUNICATIONS

The Dragon Card Dated April 28, 1970

Z32 Cipher | The Button Letter Dated June 26, 1970

This communication is sometimes known as the "Map Code" because it came with a San Francisco Bay area map. A symbol closely resembling the crosshairs image used by Zodiac to sign many of his messages appeared on the map as a compass, with the instructions "0 is to be set to Mag. N."

This is the Zodiac speaking

I have become very upset with the people of San Fran Bay Area. They have <u>not</u> complied with my wishes for them to wear some nice ⊕ buttons. I promiced to punish them if they did not comply, by anilating a full School Buss. But now school is out for the summer, so I punished them in an another way.
I shot a man sitting in a parked car with a .38.

⊕-12   SFPD-0

The Map coupled with this code will tell you whoe the bomb is set. You have untill next Fall to dig it up. ⊕

C △ J I ■ O K ⊥ A M ⊐ ▲ Ω O R T G
X ⊙ F D V ⴹ ■ H C E L ⊕ P W △

THE ZODIAC COMMUNICATIONS   lxv

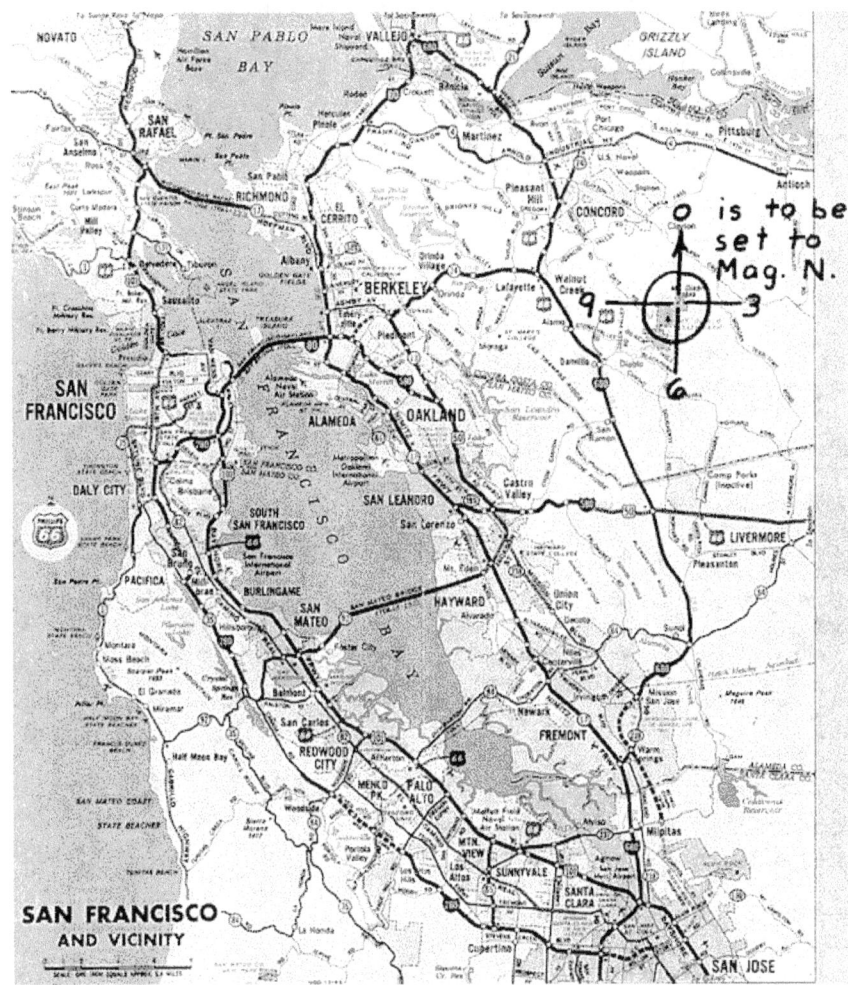

Map of San Francisco Bay area with Zodiac sign

The Kathleen Johns Letter Dated July 24, 1970

This is the Zodiac speaking

I am rather unhappy because you people will not wear some nice ⊕ buttons. So I now have a little list, starting with the woeman + her baby that I gave a rather intersting ride for a coupple howers one evening a few months back that ended in my burning her car where I found them.

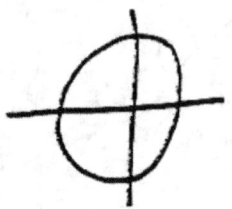

The Little List Letter | Mikado Letter Dated July 26, 1970

This is the Zodiac speaking

Being that you will not wear some nice ⊕ buttons, how about wearing some nasty ⊕ buttons. Or any type of ⊕ buttons that you can think up. If you do not wear any type of ⊕ buttons I shall (on top of every thing else) torture all 13 of my slaves that I have wateing for me in Paradice. Some I shall tie over ant hills and watch them scream + twich and sqwirm. Others shall have pine splinters driven under their nails + then burned. Others shall be placed in cages + fed salt beef untill they are goryed then I shall listen to their pleass for water and I shall laugh at them. Others will hang by their thumbs + burn in the sun then I will rub them down with deep heat to warm

| The Little List Letter Pg. 1

them up. Others I shall
stin them alive + let them
run around screaming. And
all billiard players I shall
have them play in a dark
ened dungeon all with crooked
cues & Twisted Shoes.
Yes I shall have great
fun inflicting the most
delicious of pain to my
Slaves

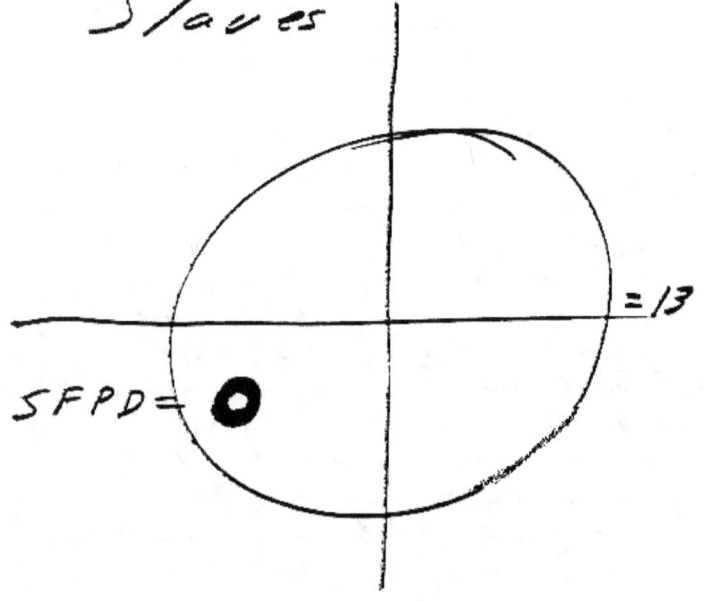

The Little List Letter Pg. 2

As some day it may hapen that a victom must be found. I've got a little list. I've got a little list, of society offenders who might well be underground who would never be missed who would never be missed. There is the pestulentual nucences who whrite for autographs, all people who have flabby hands and irritating laughs. All children who are up in dates and implore you with im platt. All people who are shakeing hands shake hands like that. And all third persons who with unspoiling take thoes who insist. They'd none of them be missed. They'd none of them be missed. There's the banjo seranader and the others of his race and the piano orginast I got him on the list. All people who eat pepermint and phomphit

| The Little List Pg. 3

in your face, they would never be missed They would never be missed And the Idiout who phrases with inthusastic tone of centuries but this and every country but his own. And the lady from the provences who dress like a guy who doesn't cry and the singurly abnomily the girl who never kissed. I don't think she would be missed Im shure she wouldn't be missed. And that nice impriest that is rather rife the judicial hummerest I've got him on the list All funny fellows, commic men and clowns of private life. They'd none of them be missed. They'd none of them be missed. And uncompromiseing kind such as wachamacallit, thingmebob, and likewise, well—nevermind, and tut tut tut tut, and whatshisname, and you know

| The Little List Pg. 4

who, but the task of filling up the blanks I rather leave up to you. But it really doesn't matter whom you place upon the list, for none of them be missed, none of them be missed.

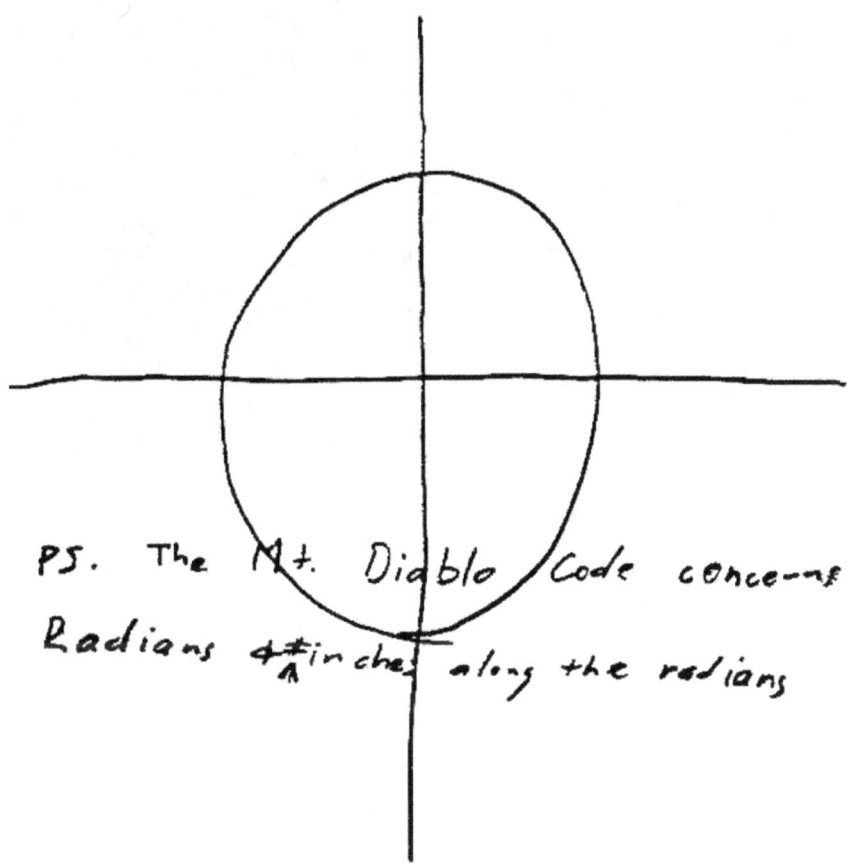

PS. The Mt. Diablo Code concerns Radians + # inches along the radians

The Little List Pg. 5

Halloween Card Dated Oct 27, 1970

The Los Angeles Times Letter Dated March 13, 1971

This is the Zodiac speaking
Like I have always said
I am crack proof. If the
Blue Meannies are ever
going to catch me, they had
best get off their fat asses
& do something. Because the
longer they fiddle & fart
around, the more slaves
I will collect for my after
life. I do have to give them
credit for stumbling across
my riverside activity, but
they are only finding the
easy ones, there are a hell
of a lot more down there.
The reason that I'm writing
to the Times is this, They
don't bury me on the back pages
like some of the others.
SFPD—0 ⊕—17+

The Sierra Club Card Dated March 22, 1971

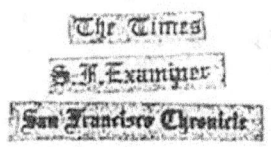

att. Paul averly = chronicke

The Exorcist Letter Dated January 29, 1974

I saw + think "The Exorcist" was the best saterical comidy that I have ever seen.

Signed, yours truley:

He plunged him self into the billowy weve and an echo arose from the sucides grave
tit willo   tit willo
    tit willo

Ps. if I do not see this note in your paper, I will do something nasty, which you know I'm capable of doing

Me - 37
SFPD - 0

The SLA Letter Dated February 14, 1974

Dear Mr. Editor,
 Did you know that the initials SLAY (Symbionese Liberation Army) spell "sla," an old Norse word meaning "kill."

a friend

The Citizen Letter Dated May 8, 1974

Sirs — I would like to express my consternation concerning your poor taste & lack of sympathy for the public, as evidenced by your running of the ads for the movie "Badlands," featuring the blurb — "In 1959 most people were killing time. Kit & Holly were killing people." In light of recent events, this kind of murder-glorification can only be deplorable at best (not that glorification of violence was <u>ever</u> justifiable) why don't you show some concern for public sensibilities & cut the ad?

     A citizen

The Red Phantom Letter Dated July 8, 1974

Editor—
Put Marco back in the hell-hole from whence it came — he has a serious psychological disorder— always needs to feel superior. I suggest you refer him to a shrink. Meanwhile, cancel the Count Marco column. Since the Count can write anonymously, so can I——

the Red Phantom
(red with rage)

The Top Secret Letter Dated May 2, 1978

Dear Channel Nine;

This is the Zodiac speaking. You people in LA are in for a treat. In the next three weeks you are finally gona have something good to report. I have decided to begin killing again — PLEASE hold the applause! Nothing is going to happen until I do. You people just won't let me have it any other way. I plan to kill five people in the next three weeks (1) Chief piggy Darrel Gates (2) Ex Chief piggy Ed Davis (3) Pat Boone — his theocratic crap is a obscenity to the rest of the world! (4) Also Eldrige Cleaver — the niggers gotta get their 20% quota — after all. And Susan Atkins — The Judas of the Manson Family. She's gona get hers now. Hey — — — you actors — this is your lucky break. Remenber — whoever plays me has his work cut out for him. See you in the News!

1. Zodiac Killer — Wikipedia. https://en.wikipedia.org/wiki/340_cypher

Ciphers And Cryptograms
INTERVIEW WITH DAVID ORANCHAK

Since the whole idea of cryptograms and ciphers can be very confusing to people, at least it is for me, we decided the next step in our investigation was to talk to an expert on codes. While watching a Zodiac mini-series on TV, I noticed one of their regular guests was an American codebreaker, David Oranchak.

The Travel Channel featured an episode on the documentary *Mysteries at the Museum* devoted to the Zodiac case. Host Don Wildman presented a basic overview of the Zodiac case and visited the four crime scenes. He also consulted with cipher expert David Oranchak. Wildman and Oranchak examined the Zodiac's first coded message,

"Z408," and the "Z340" while discussing some of the killer's methods as a cryptographer.[1]

Luckily for us, Michael Butterfield knew him and was able to get him on the show. In 2019, we had him on with other guests in a roundtable discussion about the Zodiac but dedicated one of those episodes to him.

David has a website about the Zodiac ciphers at *zodiackillerciphers.com*.

Q. There were four ciphers by the Zodiac. Maybe give us an overview of them.

A. Yes, there were four ciphers. The first cipher Zodiac mailed out, the Z408, was received by three different newspapers on August 1, 1969. The cipher was split into three parts. Zodiac also sent letters to the newspapers that included descriptions of the crimes he had committed and demanded these ciphers printed. Otherwise, he was going to go on a killing spree.

The three parts were grids of mysterious symbols, and presumably, they contained a hidden message. So, the ciphers were published, and less than a week later, a high school teacher and his wife, Donald and Bettye Harden, who had been working on the ciphers for about 20 hours, managed to crack the codes.

The Z408 ended up being a single substitution cipher. Basically, that type of cipher is when you take the letters of your message and replace them with other letters or symbols. Normally, when you do a substitution cipher, you replace the letters of your original message with just one other letter. For example, you would take all of the "Es" in your message that you are trying to hide and replace them with the letter "Z." Those were the kinds of puzzles that were common in newspapers back then. Like a crypto quote, where you would see a famous quotation from an author or celebrity, and it looked like gibberish because some of the letters were replaced with other letters. To solve it, you can look at the code and kind of figure out a common letter in the English language, such as "E." So, if you see a bunch of "Zs" in the message, then they're likely to be "Es." If you plug in "Es" for all the "Zs" and work through the words that show up or the guesses of words that show up, this process of elimination will help you guess what the code is.

However, in this cipher, Zodiac made it a little bit harder to use those kinds of clues. The high frequency of the letter "E" was hidden by the fact that Zodiac used multiple symbols to stand for the letter "E." So, instead of just replacing it with a "Z," he replaced it with seven different symbols. The challenge to a code breaker is to figure out which symbols are associated with "E," and then you can reverse the process and get the original message.

What the Hardens' did was on top of counting up the number of symbols in the ciphertext, they found patterns in the message itself. They used those patterns and certain facts about the English language. For example, the letters of "LL" are the most common letters to be placed together in a sentence, words like "shall," "will," and "kill." As it turned out, the word "kill" appeared several times in the message. The Hardens' had a hunch that the Zodiac would be talking about killing, talking about his crimes, and talking about himself. From that assumption, they made guesses about what the message would say. And through those guesses, they were able to narrow down the possible solution to that first cipher.

That's what we know about the ciphers, at least one of them was a substitution cipher, and it had a valid solution. You can check for yourself. You can take the key to it, which is just a list of which letters go with which symbols, and you replace them in the cipher. You get this long message that was written by Zodiac. But we don't know about the remaining three ciphers that he sent, what system he used, I mean.

The second cipher he sent, the Z340, looked a lot like the first one, except it was sent in one part on one page rather than three different sections. It used a lot of special symbols. Some symbols were in the first cipher, but it also had some new ones in it.

When you look at it, you think maybe he just did another substitution cipher. But, we're coming up on 50 years later, and that premise has not born any fruit. Not only did we have a lot of smart people over the years try their substitutions on the cipher, but we've also had a lot of advanced computer technology and software to attack the code as if it were a substitution cipher. So far, those attempts have failed. There must be something different about the second cipher. *(The Z340 Cipher was finally cracked by computer programmers Jarl Van Eycke, Sam Blake, and David Oranchak in December 2020.)*

Q. The first cipher, what they call the 408 because there were 408 symbols, how hard was that to construct? Do you think that it indicated some expertise or someone that looked at this as a hobby?

A. It's hard to say. I think that as popular as the crypto quotes were in those days and as an idea in pop culture, codes and ciphers were a bit more widespread back then than they are today. There were many stories about criminals and spies writing secret messages to each other, and the coded messages were commonly featured in these stories. Kids were getting decoder rings in their cereals. So, the average person could figure out how a substitution cipher worked.

The type of cipher the 408 was made it a little bit harder to solve. It was known as a "Homophonic Substitution Cipher." That's basically a little spin on the traditional substitution cipher that you would see in the newspapers. It was not that much of a stretch to learn how to do one if you already knew how to do a substitution cipher.

So, you don't really need to have that much expertise to understand how they work. Zodiac could have picked it up from something he read. But it was also possible that he learned code-making in the military and maybe had some formal training related to ciphers. It's hard to say. But I wouldn't conclude that he had to have picked it up from formal training.

Even Donald Harden, the high school teacher that solved some of the 408, was quoted in the newspaper after the solution was published, saying that he "didn't think the code itself was that sophisticated." In fact, he "thought it was from some cheap detective story somewhere."

Q. Harden, the teacher, didn't have any formal training either, did he?

A. No, he was described as having a childhood interest in codes. So, he had probably been working on puzzles for a long time and solving cryptograms. Harden didn't have any formal training by the military either, so all it took for him to solve the code was just life experience.

Q. The Zodiac also claimed that the cipher would reveal his identity, and there are 18 symbols that appear to be gibberish at the end of the message. What are your feelings about that?

A. Yes, he did make that claim that the Zodiac identity would be in there. You can argue that even though he didn't put his name in the readable part, the 390 characters, the letter was kind of a mission statement where he talked about his motivations for killing and how it made him feel. So, there was a little bit of an abstract identity, a statement, in there.

Using the key that the Hardens' found, the last 18 symbols got most of the message to decrypt into a readable message except for the last 18. But no one knows for sure what they mean. Either they were just filler since he had sent the cipher out in three parts. He could only have wanted to make them equal size. They were all in blocks of 17 characters in a row across and eight down. So, he had to complete the block in the last one to make it even. The rationale for this was that if he were trying to make it harder to crack, then he would not give them the extra clue of knowing which part might be the last. Because if you've got a message that doesn't divide equally, then you'll have the last part that's going to be smaller than the others. By putting a bunch of random symbols in, he avoided easy identification of which part was the last. There was evidence of that because a lot of the symbols were copied from patterns that appeared earlier in the ciphertext. So, that was one of the arguments for the last 18 just being just filler.

Q. What do you think of the theory that it was, in itself, another cipher or another message?

A. That's certainly an idea that had been explored very soon after the Harden solution was published in the papers. People tried to take the last 18 symbols and the last 18 letters of plain text that resulted by applying the Hardens' key, and they tried to rearrange it. So, they were using anagrams basically to rearrange the letters to see if any names came out.

Q. Like Robert Emmet the Hippie, correct?

A. Yes, like "Robert Emmet the Hippie," which wasn't even spelled right. But that didn't stop people from going through the phonebooks trying to dig up a Robert Emmets.[2] So, people have been trying anything to try and figure it out. I lean toward the last 18 just being filler. It seems like the most logical explanation, but you can't be 100 percent certain.

Q. Why wasn't the letter enough to express his feelings? Why did he also have to do these ciphers?

A. The Zodiac wanted a certain kind of attention, and the ciphers were a way to get the public to take part in it or interact with him. When he sent those first three ciphers, they were accompanied by a letter that demanded they be published. So, it was obviously very important that they were published in the newspapers at that time. It was the way he wanted it. He either wanted people running around trying to solve his puzzle, or there was some other ulterior motive involved. But I don't know what that would be.

Q. What do you say to people who suggest that the Zodiac cipher was never solved by any experts working for the government during that same period of time. And that it was just the Hardens'. Were there other people that came to the same solution? We know there was a so-called "Cipher Key" sent by someone anonymously that appeared to coincide with the ciphers. Is that correct?

A. Yes. The "Concerned Citizen Key" was received very soon after the Hardens' solution was published in the papers. So, it's impossible to know. We don't know if the concerned citizen key was independently solved and they just sent it in, or if it was sent by the killer himself because he was tired of waiting for the papers to say somebody found the answer. Maybe it was just since the papers were publishing the decoded messages, and they didn't tell anyone what symbols were associated with each letter. So, he was just doing something to try and be helpful.

When the newspapers received the ciphers, they were sent to the Vallejo police and the navy cryptographer at nearby Mare Island. But I don't know how much effort they put into them. I don't think the FBI started working on it right away. That led people to think they tried, failed, and that they couldn't crack the first cipher. But I think in the Lake Berryessa Report, there was some mention about the FBI having independently solved the 408 Cipher. And their answer matched the Hardens' answer. I think that was probably true because of the kind of code that the first cipher was. It was not that hard to break, ultimately. Compared to the wartime codes during WWII, the complexity of the codes sent back and forth, and the ones intercepted and cracked during the war, were a lot more difficult.

Q. What are the chances that all the ciphers will be solved? Why has it taken so long?

A. It takes a special kind of mind to tackle the ciphers.

Q. Why is it that so many people say they found their suspect's name in the cipher? Why isn't that strong evidence?

A. The main reason is that you can use these techniques, whatever technique you're using to come up with the names, to produce other names using the same steps. There's what I call "coincidence generators," where people will go and do things like taking anagrams of letters that appear in the ciphertext and rearranging them, so they produce a name that's similar to their suspect's name. Or, they produce some personal feature that connects them to their suspect.

They'll do things like numerology on the ciphertext where they're assigning numbers. If a symbol appears in the fourth column, they'll give it the number four. They'll do these arithmetic tricks to make it produce another name. Maybe the killer hid his birthday in the layout of the symbols somehow.

The problem with those approaches is that you can generate millions of dates using that numerological approach and an astronomical number of anagrams by rearranging the letters. You can use any key and just rearrange the result to get anything that you want. Eventually, you're going to hit something.

Q. Isn't it also that we are pattern-seeking animals? Someone was looking for Arthur Leigh Allen's name, and behold, they found it. Somebody else was looking for a certain name, and they found that one. Doesn't that play a large part of it? What your motive and your method was when you started? It has to have a lot to do with your results.

A. Yes, absolutely. That encourages confirmation bias. So, you go out and find patterns that match your suspect. A good example is Gary Stewart, and his book about Earl Van Best, his biological father, who he claims was the Zodiac. He has multiple decryptions of the cipher that finds variations of Earl Van Best's name. It could be like the initials or just parts of the name. He's only pointing out the cases where his method produces Earl Van Best's name. But if you use the same steps with a different name, you can find that one too.

That said, what if his method is valid? What if there was only one way to produce a name out of it? And it turned out to be Earl Van Best? Now, that would be compelling. But when I actually go through the steps and generate names, I can get tens of thousands of names to pop out the exact same way. The main reason is that there are so many degrees of freedom in the steps you are using that you can make it say just about anything. But if you already have the name of a suspect in mind, and you're going to ignore the other ones and only focus on the ones that match your suspect, you're going to ignore the fact that you can make Dr. Suess's name come out of the cipher.

CIPHERS AND CRYPTOGRAMS 17

Listen to the full interview with David on my website:

https://www.alanrwarren.com/hom-podcast-episodes/episode/7d16b1d2/zodiac-ciphers-david-oranchak

---

1. Blog | | ZodiacKillerFacts.com. http://zodiackillerfacts.com/blog/
2. ROBERT EMMETS — In the 8/12/69 *Chronicle* article, just a few days after the Hardens' solution to the 408 Cipher was published, it indicated that "several puzzle solvers had come up with the name "Robert Emmet" and passed it on to Vallejo Police Sergeant, John Lynch. The article indicated that Sgt. Lynch was "checking on Robert Emmets, hippie or otherwise."

Don Cheney

INTERVIEW WITH DREW HURST BEESON

During the Zodiac Killer investigation, a man by the name of Don Cheney came forward to report his friend, who he suspected to be the Zodiac. Arthur Leigh Allen (December 18, 1933 — August 26, 1992) was the prime suspect of law enforcement in the Zodiac case. Publicly, Allen became known as a Zodiac suspect shortly after the release of the book, *Zodiac*, authored by Robert Graysmith. The original case against Allen was detailed in Graysmith's book, where Graysmith laid out the circumstantial evidence against Allen using the pseudonym Bob Hall Starr to hide Allen's identity.

Later, Allen was cleared of any suspicion through a comparison of DNA, fingerprints, palm prints, and handwriting. Arthur Leigh Allen died of a heart attack in his home in Vallejo on August 26, 1992, at the age of 58.

Recently, a book about Don Cheney titled *Sighting In On The Zodiac* was written by Drew Hurst Beeson. We were fortunate to interview Beeson on the show three times in 2019 and 2020.

Drew Hurst Beeson has been exploring the unknown all his life. Inspired by *Coast-to-Coast AM* and *Unsolved Mysteries*, Drew is on a mission to understand our mysterious world. His first foray into true crime writing is his latest book, *Sighting In On The Zodiac: Unmasking America's Most Puzzling Unsolved Murders*. He is also the author of *The Cloak of the Brethren* and *Asleep in Hell*, and he hosts a true crime/conspiracy YouTube channel as well.

Drew has recently been featured on the following podcasts: *Paranormal Dimensions* with David Young of Paranormal U.K. Radio, *Conspiracy Unlimited* with Richard Syrett, *The Cooper Vortex* with Darren Schaeffer, and *Zodiac: the Most Dangerous Game* with

Herschel Norman. He has appeared on radio as a storyteller on *Coast-to-Coast AM's* annual "Ghost to Ghost" episode and as a featured guest on *Midnight in the Desert* with Dave Schrader. He is currently working on a book about the Riverside murder of Cheri Jo Bates, a book on D.B. Cooper, and a novel about missing persons.

Q. So, who was Don Cheney, and how does he relate to the Zodiac Killer?

A. For those who might not be as familiar with Don Cheney, he's the person who came forward with accusations about his long-time friend, Arthur Leigh Allen. Allen was, and probably still is, the top Zodiac Killer suspect due to Robert Graysmith's book, *Zodiac*, which later became the Fincher movie of the same title.[1]

Most of Graysmith's book is about Arthur Leigh Allen. We only know about Allen because Don Cheney came forward in the Summer of 1971 with claims that he felt his friend was the Zodiac Killer. He said he had read an article in the newspaper about one of the Zodiac letters that spoke of "picking off little kiddies who came bouncing off the bus."

According to Don Cheney, who has a pretty good memory, when he saw that in the newspaper, he remembered his friend telling him this same thing on New Years Day 1969. There's a little caveat there. When he first started telling this story, it was New Years Day 1968. But I think for his convenience, he switched that date to New Years Day 1969.

As Don's story went, he went over to his friend Arthur Leigh Allen's house, who was living in Vallejo, ground zero of the Zodiac crimes. Cheney claimed that Allen was telling him how he wanted to become a killer for a living and not work a regular job. He wouldn't need a resume for that, and he was going to call himself the Zodiac. He was going to hunt people on "lover's lanes." Supposedly, he told all of this to Don.

It took Don two and a half years to come forward with this information. So, that's how he enters the whole scene. He inserted himself into this case. He was a friend of Arthur Leigh Allen's through Allen's younger brother, Ron Allen, a college roommate of Don Cheney at Cal-poly in Pomona, California, close to Los Angeles. They remained friends for about eight years.

Q. Did you have any interaction with Don Cheney yourself?

A. Absolutely not. Don Cheney passed away in 2009, and I never had any interaction with him whatsoever.

Q. What kind of a person do you think Don Cheney was?

A. Well, I could tell that he was more intelligent than what he let on. It interested me that he was an engineer. People thought he was a civil engineer, but he was actually a mechanical engineer. More specifically, he worked as a pipe stress analyst for a company after leaving the Bay area. I thought it was intriguing because one of the Zodiac letters talks about radian in the Mount Diablo area, and the concept of radian is definitely something a mechanical engineer is going to be familiar with. I felt that his background as a mechanical engineer well suited what was in a lot of the Zodiac letters, not just ciphering and the mathematical component, but all of it.

Here you have somebody who is pretty organized in thought. Not only was that a good fit but a lot of his phrasings I picked up on. He did a sit-down interview with Tom Voigt in 2001, and Tom put the transcript up on his website. I noticed a lot of phrases that Don Cheney used were seen repeated in quite a bit of the Zodiac correspondence, such as the word "bouncing." Don used that word a lot. He talked about Arthur Leigh Allen being in the Navy for a while, and Don responded with, "Yes, he was. Until they bounced him out." Don used many phrases that the

Zodiac did. Another one was "a slip of the tongue." You see that phrase in the "Concerned Citizen Letter." It's attributed to the Zodiac. When Don Cheney was in the interview with Tom Voigt, he used that phrase when he talked about being polygraphed on his involvement in this case.

Q. Now, Michael (Butterfield), you've interviewed Don Cheney before, haven't you?

A. (Michael) Yes, several times back in 2006. He had already talked to Tom Voigt and Robert Graysmith, and I think he had talked a little bit with the movie producers. But they hadn't filmed that interview for the documentary. When I contacted him, I was hoping he would be credible and that it would all make sense. I was hoping he would clear up a lot of issues and discrepancies so that we could accept his story. No one wanted to believe that somebody would make up a story like that. It would be a lot easier if he told the truth because that would mean Allen was probably the Zodiac, and the case had been solved. So, I was really hoping he would explain these things and clear up some of these issues. Instead, what he did shocked me repeatedly, time and again. He embellished his stories and told brand new stories, some of which seemed to be based on erroneous information he was getting from Robert Graysmith's book.

So, he was taking the book, and like many people assuming the stories in it were true. Then, he would take one of these stories and embellish it without understanding that the story had no basis in fact in the first place. One of those stories was, and Drew is probably familiar with this, the infamous painting party at the home of the Zodiac victim, Darlene Ferrin.

Cheney claimed that Darlene Ferrin was being stalked by somebody. We should say for the listeners that they didn't name Arthur Leigh Allen in the book. Graysmith referred to him as "Bob Hall Star." Later on,

Cheney insinuated that it was by this person named Bob. Then, there's this story about a painting party at Darlene Ferrin's home. In the book, it said that a man named Ron Allen attended this party. Of course, Ron Allen is Arthur Leigh Allen's younger brother. Don Cheney read the book, saw that story, and then started recounting how Ron and Karen, his wife, had gone to this party using details from the book, like saying they were there with Arthur Leigh Allen. When I spoke to Karen Allen, she told me that neither she nor her husband had ever been to that party, and they had never told Don Cheney that story. They also didn't believe that Don Cheney was telling the truth.

There's another story that Arthur Leigh Allen attempted to molest one of Don Cheney's children. Ron Allen had reported this to police, and when they talked to him, he said, "Don Cheney had confronted me about this situation." The Allen family believed that it played a part in Don Cheney inventing these stories.

So, when I spoke to Cheney, I was hoping he would straighten things out. Instead, he made a much bigger mess. He claimed that he never told police and that he remembered later on that Arthur Leigh Allen took him to the crime scene at Lake Berryessa to show him where the murder occurred. He claimed Allen told him that he had been hired to kill Darlene Ferrin by Darlene's husband and that Darlene's husband was a drug dealer who had a front business using vending machines to cover up his drug business. None of which was true. So, it just became more and more complicated, and by the time he appeared in the documentary, one of the Vallejo police officers came right out and said, "I don't trust this guy anymore."

That was a real turning point in things. And what Drew was talking about before is important because Don Cheney said the conversation with Allen, where he allegedly made those incriminating statements, occurred in December 1967 or January 1968. But then, years later, Cheney was questioned about it, and he claimed that

Arthur Leigh Allen had also mentioned losing his teaching job during that conversation. In fact, Allen lost that job in March of 1968, which was after when he claimed the conversation took place. When he found out about that discrepancy, he changed his story to a year later.

Q. So, Drew, do you have that feeling as well? Did you get that feeling that he wasn't a very trustworthy person?

A. (Drew) Absolutely. He said a lot of things that contradicted himself. Over the years, he changed his story. The molestation attempt story is important because many people will say that Don made up lies, probably because he was mad about the incident with his daughter. Don Cheney had one daughter and a son. If you go by the date his daughter was born, in late '64, she would have been around 3-years old, or 3½ at the time of the assault. That was kind of young even for Arthur Leigh Allen, compared to the age he was going for when he got in trouble as a teacher at Valley Springs. The kids were a little closer to 9 or 10-years old. There are no reports of Allen going for someone that young at all. The incident was described as the daughter came forward and told them that Uncle Leigh touched her bottom, not a full-fledged attack but some sort of touching incident. Don was mad about that, so he tried to get revenge. It's pretty obvious that the incident probably never really happened. It was just concocted for some reason to shift the blame over to Allen.

I know that Tom Voigt interviewed Cheney's daughter as an adult, and she claimed it never happened. It was never reported to the police. But you're right in that he did say something to Ron Allen about it. It doesn't hold any water, though. Even with Don's admission, he stayed friends with Allen for six months and up to a year and a half after this alleged incident with his daughter.

Arthur Leigh Allen was a child molester. Nobody denies that, but the incident with Don's daughter is making Arthur Leigh

Allen the perfect patsy for the Zodiac crimes.

A. (Michael Butterfield) It's possible that nothing happened, but Don Cheney believed that it did happen. Because he didn't have absolute proof, he didn't end their relationship. It seems clear that when he confronted Ron Allen about it, he was pretty upset. So, whatever really happened, I don't think we're ever really going to know. He supposedly said that he stopped hanging around Allen because he was so disturbed by those comments he made about wanting to kill people. It's interesting that he molested one of your children, and that wasn't enough to end your friendship. But when he alluded to maybe murdering people, that was enough.

Cheney was a problematic person all around, whether you believe he was involved or not. Or whether you think Allen was the Zodiac or not. In any scenario, Don Cheney had a credibility issue.

A. (Drew) Yes, Cheney had a heavy credibility issue. I always go back to the statement about licking the stamps. There were these stories about kids in the neighborhood who would lick stamps for Arthur Leigh Allen. I've never seen where that actually came from. I've never seen an interview with the kids from the neighborhood. But I always wondered why Don would have said that? Obviously, it came out when they were testing DNA on the 1969 letter sent to the *San Francisco Chronicle,* and Don was worried.

Why would he say that? If it was just to pin it on Arthur Leigh Allen, he knew they were not going to find his DNA on them. But if he said, "I licked the stamps for him," the natural reaction was going to be, "Let's get a sample of your DNA." If you're sure you were licking his stamps, then they are going to find your DNA. Other than the fear that his DNA was going to show up, there's no reason for Don to make that statement.

Q. It's interesting how the stories about the licking stamps only came out after it was publicized that they were testing for DNA. How did the police handle Don Cheney? Did they investigate him? What were their findings if they did?

A. He wasn't looked at that closely until Vallejo Detective George Bawart took over the case. That's when Don made the statement about licking the stamps. It was after they started to focus on him. His DNA was tested. I don't know exactly when, but it was negative. So was Arthur Leigh Allen's and everyone else's who had ever been tested. Plus, they found that the DNA came from outside of the stamp, which kind of put everything back in place as far as DNA went in this case. For that matter, Arthur Leigh Allen is back in play. If you can't definitively say it came from the back of the stamp, we're still in play.

Most people know that the DNA with the San Francisco Police Department is pretty weak, with only 4 out of 9 markers. Vallejo was trying to develop a DNA profile a couple of years ago, but they never came out to say they were successful in doing so.

That comment about the stamps did put him on the radar of Detective Bawart, though. It led to Don Cheney taking a polygraph test. Don was living in Washington State at the time. They set up the first polygraph for him in Seattle, and someone from the FBI came in to make sure that it was done right. Don's response was to get extremely drunk the day before the test was scheduled. When he came in, he was so hungover that he couldn't take the polygraph. Knowing he had the test the next day, why did he choose to get drunk? He was obviously worried about something. So, the test was administered later, and the results were inconclusive, to the best of my knowledge. When you combine the thumbprint, the DNA comment, and the fact he got really drunk the day before his scheduled polygraph, it shows he was either not telling the truth about Allen, or he had some involvement in the case. There's a lot of smoke there.

Q. You mentioned Detective Bawart. He was the Detective in the documentary that said he questioned Cheney's credibility?

A. Absolutely.

Q. As a person, what would make you think that Don Cheney would not only be a killer but the Zodiac Killer?

A. He's got an odd personality. He liked to cover his intelligence, much like the Zodiac did in his letters by misspelling words when obviously he wasn't a bad speller because you found the same words spelled correctly somewhere else. Plus, Don knew Arthur Leigh Allen misspelled words, and he knew that would be a good backdrop.

Don was estranged from his family. He stayed married to his wife, but his family moved to the east coast when his daughter was probably 13, and his son was about 11. They lived on separate coasts. Even when they were married, and his children were younger, he was never really around. He was never able to hold a job. Despite being trained as a mechanical engineer, he was always job-hopping. I don't know exactly what was going on with the jobs, not sure if it was a problem with authority, but there was something going on. He was always trying to make a living. He had numerous jobs: he sold insurance for a while, and he was going to a lot of different power plants looking for work. So, he had some anger or some isolation issues.

Q. If Don Cheney were the Zodiac, why wouldn't he have tried to frame Arthur Leigh Allen with some evidence?

A. That's one of the most common questions I get, "Why wouldn't Don Cheney leave a piece of Paul Stine's shirt at Allen's place, or something like that? Or one of the weapons?" My only response is that Don Cheney didn't want Arthur Leigh Allen to go down as the Zodiac Killer. Because then the game would be over, and he would not be able to live through the crimes he committed anymore. The Zodiac moniker was probably bigger to him than the crime scenes themselves: creating the person and the elaborate costume. I love starting with Lake Berryessa. It's ground zero for me because Bryan Hartnell is such a great witness. He really engaged in a conversation. Bryan is so sharp, and he's a probate attorney now. He had a good presence of mind when this was going on. It's a good starting point for all things pointing to him. But my point is that Don didn't want the game to be over.

You have to wonder why Arthur Leigh Allen is still the number one suspect to this day. It's because the evidence against him is so solid.

UPDATE ON DON CHENEY BY DREW BEESON

A few months later, Drew came back on the show and discussed some new information on his suspect, Don Cheney.

Q. So, what new information did you find out about Don Cheney?

A. Well, when I was doing some more research, I found out that Don Cheney was in the air force, and I never knew that before. He was in the air force for two years.

For people who research the Zodiac, you will recall the Wing Walker shoe print left at the Lake Berryessa attack. Wing Walker is an air force shoe for people who work on planes because it had a non-slip sole and steel toes.

Another reason this is important is that the Zodiac has always been tied to the military. In the military, he may have received cryptology training. So, people always think the Zodiac must have been in the military or was ex-law enforcement.

Listen to the full interviews with Drew on my website:

https://www.alanrwarren.com/hom-podcast-episodes/episode/aae452ca/sighting-in-on-the-zodiac-drew-beeson

https://www.alanrwarren.com/hom-podcast-episodes/episode/b690c0cf/drew-hurst-beeson-zodiac-killer

https://www.alanrwarren.com/hom-podcast-episodes/episode/cf3675fc/drew-beeson-zodiac-killer-update-2020

1. Don Cheney met Arthur Leigh Allen in 1962 and maintained a friendship with him through 1968. Their friendship ended in 1969, after a New Year's Day conversation in which Allen spoke of killing at random and called himself "Zodiac." Cheney soon moved to the Los Angeles area and eventually came forward to the police after reading a quote in a newspaper article that spurred his memory. The quote was of the Zodiac Killer's threat to shoot out a school bus's tires and kill the children inside. Just months earlier, Cheney realized, Allen had talked of doing the same thing. (Don Cheney Speaks | Zodiac Killer | Zodiac Murders | The .... https://www.zodiackiller.com/Cheney.html)

Joseph James DeAngelo Jr.
INTERVIEW WITH ANNE PENN

Who was Joseph James DeAngelo Jr., a.k.a. "The Golden State Killer," a.k.a. "Visalia Ransacker," a.k.a. "East Area Rapist," a.k.a. "Original Night Stalker?" Who else was he as he traveled through time? Was he the Zodiac Killer, too, who terrorized us in the 1960s?

Joseph James DeAngelo Jr. is a former police officer who committed at least 13 murders, 50 rapes, and 120 burglaries across California between 1973 and 1986. DeAngelo was responsible for at least three crime sprees throughout California, each spawning a different nickname in the press before it became evident the same offender committed them. In the San

Joaquin Valley, he was known as the "Visalia Ransacker" before moving to the Sacramento area, where he became known as the "East Area Rapist." The MO linked him to additional attacks in Contra Costa County, Stockton, and Modesto. DeAngelo committed serial murders in Santa Barbara, Ventura, and Orange counties, where he was known as the "Night Stalker," and later, the "Original Night Stalker." DeAngelo is believed to have taunted and threatened his victims and police in obscene phone calls and possibly written communications.[1]

To find out who he was and if he might have also been the Zodiac Killer, we contacted Author and researcher Anne Penn for an interview. Ms. Penn has been writing all of her life. Her interests are focused primarily on true stories. She has also written other books using her real name, about helping women and girls. The subject of her other books includes verbal and domestic abuse, as well as women's issues. Ms. Penn also wrote four books about the Golden State Killer case to document possible murders that are still unsolved or are now cold cases. Her background is in Psychology, Sociology, Criminal Justice, and Addiction Specialties. A Certified Addiction

Specialist, she has counseled those with substance abuse and addiction issues. She is also a certified crisis and suicide prevention counselor. We did two interviews with Anne Penn: one in 2019 and the other in 2020.

Q. How did you get into the Golden State Killer case enough to write a book about it?

A. Well, it certainly wasn't something I had thought I would ever write about because it was a story that was too scary for me. The East Area Rapist came to Sacramento in '76, apparently, at least that's the story that has been told. I lived there and grew up there. I was born at Mayfair Air Force base, and I lived there at the age of 19 to 21 when he was attacking all over Sacramento. I worked downtown, so it was a really scary time.

A couple of years later, there was a family connection; two of the murder victims were my grandfather's son and his daughter-in-law. It was one of those things that I kept in the back mind sealed off for years and years because I had some post-traumatic stress over how horrific that particular story was. I was always afraid of sliding glass doors and all the stuff that happened when the East Area Rapist terrorized Sacramento. I was fortunate not to be harmed then. He hit about a minute away from my apartment off Piedmont, one of the last attacks before he was supposed to have left Sacramento. That, in a nutshell, is how the stories were tucked away in my own fear. I wanted to address that fear and try to help discover who did this in Sacramento because they had finally tied them together.

Q. So, how did you connect the Zodiac Killer with the Golden State Killer?

A. It's where the story led. I was probably more surprised than some that I ended up where I ended up. I wrote a book last year about the Golden State Killer called *The Creep Among Us* because I knew he was in Sacramento and thought that's where we would find him. I profiled him myself and worked with Larry Compton. So, I ended up with two books. First, I was trying to find him and also honor new victims. The second book was to inform people about what other murders he might have committed. The third one, the newest book, *What If,* was about what was going on with the case. I am a very curious person, so I checked into what other murders might have occurred around that time and place. Just like many sleuths have over time, many people thought he was a cop. That was my main focus when I started this book: could we tie him to other murders? Were there other victim's families out there that would be happy with finding answers at this late date?

Q. You believe they have the right guy? DeAngelo? As far as the Golden State Killer, correct?

A. I do. There was a 100 percent DNA match. I also add alleged. You have to because he hasn't been convicted in a court of law yet. But 100 percent DNA match to all the different crime scenes where he left his DNA doesn't give him much wiggle room.

Q. With the Golden Stake Killer, they were able to match the DNA he left behind at the murder scenes. Do you think they will be able to match him with that same DNA to the Zodiac murders?

A. No. From every report I've heard, they attempted to. But they could not get a good enough DNA profile or sample to rule him in or out. I kept waiting for that to occur because, in 2014, or '15, one of the first things I did was look at the Zodiac as possibly being the East Area Rapist or Golden State Killer, just because of his geography involved. As well, he seemed like he could be in the military or on a police force. When I read about some of the things the Zodiac did, I was hoping that the man who was the Golden State Killer was younger. I just thought that he was. Zodiac was too young to be the same guy. I was off by about five to eight years in my estimation. So, I dropped the theory Zodiac was the Golden State Killer and went after investigating full-time into the East Area

Rapist or the Original Night Stalker, which is what we called him then.

Q. So, what was the first thing that drew you back to DeAngelo being the Zodiac?

A. Well, what occurred was investigating and seeing the kinds of things this person was doing. You cannot prove that somebody was the person who poisoned dogs. You cannot prove that he was the burglar that broke in everywhere. What you can see are patterns of behavior: geographically, chronologically, and what you can see is after there were dog poisonings and killings, there were also burglaries.

You could see these clustered attacks and someone who hit there and moved on to someplace else. Then, you see the same thing that happened in another geographical area, where they killed dogs, and they did the recon, and then they did the burglaries, and they went on from there.

Other crimes were occurring at the same time, like peeping and prowling, and just malicious stuff. Games this person was playing. You can see patterns over time and geographic area that tied to or had possible connections to DeAngelo.

Q. Do we know if DeAngelo lived in San Francisco or in that area?

A. There are ties to it. His father was stationed at Hamilton Airforce Base (Marin County) in Van Nuys, and Vallejo, and that area. Then, Presidio in San Francisco. So, he could have gone in that direction with his own family member. Certainly, if he lived in Auburn or the Sacramento area, he went to Folsom High School. He had to have traveled around California and Northern California. The geography, I think, is most important in proving where he was and how he did what he did.

Q. What is the most compelling thing about DeAngelo, or the thing that convinced you?

A. What was interesting to me is what happened with a lot of people who have looked at Zodiac and Golden State Killer separately as we all did. But the geography really does tell us a lot about where this guy came from and where he went. Again, during his travels, he liked to drive and hit places, and drive again, and hit again. There are incidents where on the same day, within 12 hours, he'd go from one place and hit, then go somewhere else, and hit.

So, if you go back to 1963, where you see the murders of Robert Domingos and Linda Edwards down on Gaviota Beach, then, think years later that they may be tied to the Zodiac, it might be pre-Zodiac activity. There's just all this evidence that you find.

And then, other murders happened after that, and they were of couples each time. The similarity is that DeAngelo was killing couples over time as well, and that was his objective.

So, there's just a lot of similarities between the two as far as motive and geography. I can connect him to Anna Maria at that same time in 1963. So, there's a lot of evidence that connects him to an area like Riverside, California.

Q. What do you have that connects DeAngelo to that crime?

A. He had relatives who lived in each area geographically, so he was able to do what he did and had a place to go. A lot of murders happened at the beach in 1963 and '64, and all of a sudden, he stopped. Why? Because he got into the Navy. You can easily fit the timelines, and I have yet to find an opportunity where he wasn't available. For instance, a lot of people say, "He couldn't have killed Cheri Jo Bates because he was on a ship." Well, he was docked, actually. He wasn't out to sea. He was available for that murder, and he had connections to Riverside.

Q. So, you believe DeAngelo is a suspect in the Bates murder case?

A. I believe that if he is the Zodiac, then yes.

Q. There is some DNA in the Bates case that can be tested. They have DNA from hairs found in her hand, and it was used 20 years ago to exclude a suspect they've had for years. The DNA didn't match. So it is possible to check that DNA against DeAngelo's DNA.

A. You would hope, yes, and I kept waiting. When they arrested DeAngelo, I thought, sooner or later, they would either rule him in or rule him out. I was waiting for an announcement of some sort. Meanwhile, I was still looking into what other murders he might have committed.

Q. Quite often, people say these two killers, Zodiac and DeAngelo, had different MOs.

A. Here's the thing, Joseph DeAngelo is probably the most at ease of anybody I've ever seen, and I've studied serial killers since 1980. He was able to outsmart everybody for a very long time. He had a criminal justice degree, and he was a cop. He had studied how to be a better criminal.

What he did was change his MO whenever he wanted to. I always say that his MO was fluid and moved back and forth. That's because he really wasn't tied to any one way of killing. He would also go back and forth between killing couples and lone women. There were abductions, murder scenes in vehicles, and murder scenes in homes. So, he was more fluid and able to change what he did, and he liked to play games with the cops from the beginning.

There are more things similar about the two than different, including the things he said to the victims when he committed crimes.

Q. Exactly, what do you mean by "things he said to the victims?"

A. Well, for example, everything was "I'm going to need your money," or "your car keys," and "I just need to get to Mexico," or "I need to get to Bakersfield." The things he said to the victims were identical to make them think he wasn't going to hurt them.

The way he hogtied them the same way and left them on their bellies like that. Same thing. If you study the Golden State Killer cases, and you look at what the Zodiac did, and how he treated his victims, and what he said to them, it's really the same. Even the things he wrote to the newspapers. One of the things he sent in was, "See you in the news!" If you look at the East Area Rapist when he was running amok, he wrote, "See you in the press or on TV." They both wrote poems to the news.

Q. What about when the Zodiac wore that outfit and the fact that he sent ciphers. That's quite a different behavior from the Golden State Killer, isn't it?

A. Well, he still had his little outfit in both cases. Let's just pretend that we know DeAngelo was Zodiac. The reality was that he got out of the service, and just a few months later, in the San Francisco Bay area, and he's the Zodiac. He had this outfit by the time he got to Berryessa. If you look at DeAngelo and what he did over time, he stole wigs, and he used disguises. He used every conceivable trick in the book: mustache/no mustache, gained weight/lost weight, used his left hand/used his right hand. He did everything in the world to change whatever his description was.

Q. The Zodiac disguise just seemed more elaborate, more thought out.

A. Well, he was younger then. Think about it. He was 23 versus when he was the other MO and the other monikers. He was older. So, he did change it up over time, and that's not surprising. One of the things Zodiac did, and also DeAngelo, in my opinion, was he called from a phone booth or somewhere close to the police station. DeAngelo liked to taunt the police as well. He did stuff right in the backyard of the Auburn police department. In one murder in 2003, the young lady was found a block and a half from the Auburn police department in the bushes off the sidewalk. That was a long time after the Golden State Killer supposedly stopped. But he was still there in the Auburn area. He lived right there in the attack zone, and that never seemed to stop him. There were a couple of murders in Granite Bay Springs, and they've never found the murderer.

Q. So, you think he did a lot more murders than what he is in prison for?

A. I do. After the Paul Stine murder, Zodiac said that he wasn't going to announce his kills anymore. They were going to look like accidents or revenge. He used every kind of way to kill, like starting fires. I found evidence of that as well. The day he was arrested for shoplifting or sighted for shoplifting in 1979, I went looking for an article somewhere to see what kind of rage he might be in because he was a cop, and he was arrested. Low and behold, there was an article about a house burned to the ground just down the street from Auburn. There had been items taken out of the house, and you could tell it was arson. It was in the same town that Bonnie Colwell's family lived, on Colwell Street. He liked to play games with names and people, so I'm pretty sure that he had something to do with that.

Listen to the full interviews with Anne on my website:

https://www.alanrwarren.com/hom-podcast-episodes/episode/dd5ede54/anne-penn-what-if-golden-state-killer-zodiac-solved

https://www.alanrwarren.com/hom-podcast-episodes/episode/7c79ed2d/anne-penn-end-game

1. List of fugitives from justice who disappeared-WikiMili....https://wikimili.com/en/List_of_fugitives_from_justice_who_disappeared

Earl Van Best Jr
INTERVIEW WITH GARY L. STEWART

In 2014, Gary L.Stewart published a book, *The Most Dangerous Animal of All,* in which he claimed his search for his biological father, Earl Van Best, Jr., led him to conclude Van Best was the Zodiac Killer. In 2020, the book was adapted by FX Network as a documentary series.[1]

Stewart hails from Baton Rouge, Louisiana, and currently works as an electrical engineer and Vice President of Delta Tech Service of Louisiana. As a child, he was given up for adoption and had no contact with his birth parents until his late 30s. It was then that his birth mother, Judy Gilford, reached out to him. She told Stewart that she had him when she was just a teenager and had run away from home with Earl Van Best Jr., a 27-year-old rare book dealer.[2]

The two abandoned their month-old son in Baton Rouge, leading Stewart to be adopted by another family. Learning all of this, Stewart decided to find his birth father, which led him to uncover Best. Stewart appeared on the show in the Winter of 2015.

Q. What led you to not only researching this case but also to write a book about it?

A. Well, until about 13, nearly 14-years ago now, I was just a guy who was born, raised, and lived almost all of my life here in South Louisiana. In what was a typical southern home, except for the fact that I was adopted. I always wondered why or how I came to be adopted. Here in the state of Louisiana, adoption records have been sealed since the '70s. So, I didn't have anything, not as much as a name to begin searching for. I feel very fortunate that my biological mother had the wherewithal to investigate herself and track me down about 14-years ago.

Q. What was the first thing that you asked your biological mother when you met her?

A. I flew out to meet her a couple of weeks after she contacted me, and that's when I decided to ask who my father was, what happened, why they did not stay together, and why I came available for adoption. She said, "Well, honey, you know it's been so many years ago, and I've been forced to try and forget everything about my life with you and your father. So, my memory is vague at best. I think your father's name was Van, and he was like twice my age, and we were on the run from California." Because she was 13, and he was 27, it was statutory rape at that point.

After about a year and a half on the run, after escaping from juvenile hall, and my father bonding out of jail, they ended up in New Orleans. My mother had me in New Orleans. My mother told me she thought I was about three months old when my father woke up one morning and took me by train to Baton Rouge, about 50 minutes northwest of New Orleans. By train, it was an hour and a half or so. He exited the train with me, walked about two blocks up the street in downtown Baton Rouge, and left me, abandoned in an apartment building. It was an eightplex at the time, and nobody was home. He laid me on the stairwell and walked away. That was about 11 a.m., and one of the tenants came home at 4:30 p.m. and saw me crying in the stairwell.

Of course, they did an investigation here in Baton Rouge. My footprints didn't match any of the babies in any hospital. My father was a genius, so he was smart enough to get me just far enough away from New Orleans, to where he wouldn't get caught. My mother didn't quite tell me that story. She said that he took you to Baton Rouge and turned you over to the authorities at a church so that you would be adopted. I told her then that I didn't think that I wanted to meet this guy. I have a great dad in Baton Rouge. I told her that I was not going to search for him.

That only lasted for a couple of weeks before curiosity got the best of me. I felt obligated to find him. At that point, he would have been 69-years old, and I would have loved to have heard his side of the story. But the main reason I wanted to find him was so that he could see me. And if he was carrying around any guilt or grief, like my mother said she had been for about 40 years, to allow him to let that go and be forgiven.

Q. Was your biological mother supportive in your search for your father?

A. She was living in San Francisco at the time, and I had just taken a job in the Bay area. So, I would see her at least two or three times a year. We had a real good relationship for about 12 years until I stumbled upon this horrific conclusion that I believe my father was the Zodiac Killer. At first, she was 100 percent supportive. But then later, when the book was published, she had friends of her second husband who came out and made her have second thoughts about her support of my position in my book.

As it turns out, my mother was 15 when she had me, so they were on the run for almost two years. She spent some time in a southern California correctional center for wayward girls. My father spent three years in San Quentin.

Eleven years after her life with me and my father, she remarried a very public figure in the city of San Francisco, Rotea Gilford, who became San Francisco's first-ever African-American Homicide Inspector. Then, he became the Deputy Mayor, under Dianne Feinstein and Willie Brown. My mother lived quite the high society lifestyle in San Francisco as the wife of this great figure.

Q. Wasn't he the investigator on the Zodiac Killer case as well?

A. Yes. I didn't know that Rotea was an investigator on the Zodiac case. I had no idea. I had never heard of the Zodiac Killer. When my research led me to believe that my father being the Zodiac was the only conclusion, that's when everybody sort of went underground. Rotea's family objected to my writing the book because if everything I produced to the SFPD was accurate, they felt that his reputation would be tarnished as a Zodiac inspector. My biological father and his wife's first husband being implicated as the Zodiac Killer would tarnish his reputation.

When, in fact, I take issue with that because I would have loved to have met Rotea Gilford. I wished my mother had not chosen to wait until he was deceased before she contacted me. I don't know, but there's certainly speculation about his involvement in the Zodiac investigation. That was one of the first things that got the attention of the homicide inspector I met with in 2004. But I don't know the connection, and I don't know whether my mother's second husband Rotea had any idea in the '60s about my father or what his criminal future became.

Q. What do you know about your father's history?

A. My father had an evil history long before my mother. He married a young girl once before my mother. My mother and father married in 1962. My father married a young lady, who was 17 at the time in 1957, and that marriage lasted a year. She was granted a divorce from him on the grounds of inhuman treatment and extreme cruelty. I also found out that my father was institutionalized. I knew from his transcripts from his high school that he missed a semester. His very first girlfriend reached out to me after the book was published. She told me that there was an incident involving his mother, and it had to do with something at a church. My father turned 18 in a mental institute. So, he had a history of violence and mental issues from early on.

Q. So, is your mother not accepting what you have written in the book?

A. She told me that "If I had known that your father was the Zodiac Killer, I would have never come searching for you because I wouldn't want to subject you to that sort of evil." But she also said that her second husband Rotea, and the chief of police Earl Sanders, working the Zodiac case, would often sit and talk about the Zodiac case at their home, at dinner, with family around. I can't help but wonder, maybe Rotea did a background check on his wife and found out she had this past with a pedophile, that she had a child with a pedophile. What if his name came up? Allegedly, around 1,625 men in the San Francisco area were considered Zodiac suspects at the time. Could he have interviewed him and unwittingly cleared him? But I would never blame him for being a bad cop.

Q. What was the first thing that led you to your father being the Zodiac Killer?

A. At first, when I decided I would find out who my father was, I didn't know about his police record. My mother went to the San Francisco Police Department, friends that were coworkers with her deceased husband, and it took them six months to come up with his file. They gave me a name, a social security number, and a date of birth. But they warned me that there were things in the file they would not be willing to share with me.

I really didn't care at the time. I figured he was still alive, and I had a name and social security number, so I was going to find him. I went searching on my own and ultimately found out, soon after that, he had died in 1984. But I found out that he had three other children with another lady who was from Austria. My half-siblings were now in Austria. One of them was a judge on the Republic of Austria Federal Asylum Bureau.

I also found newspaper articles about my parents' romance. It was called the "Ice Cream Romance," and it was plastered all over the newspapers' front page. This was before the Mansons, before the Zodiac, and before anything was going on in the bay area.

I went to my mother and told her I needed to get a copy of that file. So she went to Harold Butler, who was in Internal Affairs at the time. He told my mother that what was in my father's criminal file was so heinous it would destroy me. I also found out that SFPD didn't keep files on people for more than 30 years unless they were murder suspects. Well, they still have my father's file, and it's been more than 30 years.

So, at that time, I decided to give it up and forget about it and move on. Several months later, I was watching a crime show on a serial killer with Bill Curtis. They flashed the wanted poster from 1969, and the hair stood up on the back of my neck because I had seen that picture before. The SFPD didn't give me my father's criminal file, but what they gave me was the mugshot from his 1962 statutory rape of my mother. It was an identical match. The description that was written on the wanted poster fit my father perfectly.

That night, I emailed my mother and the Detective in Internal Affairs, Harold Butler, and told them that I knew what was so heinous. My father was the unsolved Zodiac Killer. My mother responded, saying, "Oh God, I hope that's not true." Harold Butler responded to my mother, "Tell Gary not to worry. His father wasn't the Zodiac Killer. The Zodiac Killer, we know who he was. He died ten years ago. We got his DNA from a piece of brain material after he passed away, and the DNA says he's the Zodiac Killer."

He was referring to Arthur Leigh Allen, of course, San Francisco's only suspect after all of these 50 years. But then I got on the internet and found out that wasn't the case at all. In 2002 or 2003, ABC's *Primetime with John Quinones* did a special on the Zodiac Killer. They were able to extract a 5-marker profile from one of the stamps on one of the letters that the Zodiac Killer sent to the *Chronicle*. Based on that 5-marker match and the genetic profile they developed on Arthur Leigh Allen's brain material, he was excluded as the Zodiac suspect because if one of those markers doesn't match, then it is not the same person.

My latest update on technology is that there are 16 markers, and if five markers match, then there's a good possibility that the candidate is still in the running. But that candidate cannot be excluded. Well, Arthur Leigh Allen and the other Zodiac suspects that someone had provided their DNA to, Sydney Holt in the SFPD Crime Lab, were all examined, and they were all excluded as being possible Zodiac suspects.

I contacted Lt. John Hennessy, head of the Homicide Unit in the SFPD in 2004. I asked him if the Zodiac case was closed, and he said no. It's not solved, far from it. He wanted me to write down my story and send it to him at the Hall of Justice, so I did. About two weeks later, I went in to see Hennessy, and he swabbed me for my DNA and told me that he was going to send it to the lab on the QT, as he was not supposed to spend any more money on the Zodiac case. There was also a backlog of cases that needed their DNAs run, so he told me it was going to take a while. I waited patiently until one day I called, and I found out that Hennessy had retired. He stopped returning my phone calls and emails. He wouldn't respond to me.

Q. What is the most compelling evidence that the Zodiac Killer was your dad?

A. Two things. Number one, the Zodiac Killer gained infamy by never getting caught and taunting the Bay area newspapers with ciphers, these cryptic word and symbol puzzles. The first one he sent was decoded. It was cracked immediately by this high school teacher and his spouse. He wrote a letter saying, "Please print the cipher on the front page of your newspaper. If not, I will go on a killing rampage on Friday, August 1st."

The Zodiac had written to the *Chronicle* on significant dates of my father and mother and my life with them. Every date that the Zodiac wrote and demanded some kind of action corresponded with the Ice Cream

Romance. That's because Paul Avery[3] was the guy who basically humiliated a want-to-be businessman, my father. Then seven years later, he came back and was targeted by this Zodiac Killer. All of those references in the newspaper articles about the Ice Cream Romance coincided with the dates the Zodiac sent Paul Avery and the *San Francisco Chronicle* his communications.

The first cipher he sent was decoded, and it had a hidden message in it that said something like, "I like killing humans or man because it's more fun than killing wild animals in the forest. After all, man is the most dangerous animal of all."[4] But what the authorities failed to do was find his name somewhere in the cipher. He said in that first letter, "If you crack this cipher, you will have my identity." They cracked the cipher by getting that message, but they didn't look close enough to the letters and symbols in the cipher solution.

In those first ciphers, my father's name E V Best Jr., is all over that cipher. I believe that the authorities and Avery had forgotten about my father by then. They had something real to write about. Avery was scared. He was targeted, and he was trying to stay underground because this madman was threatening him. I think he forgot all about Earl Van Best Jr., Judy Chandler, and the Ice Cream Romance from 1962, seven years prior.

There were three specific different ciphers, the 340 Cipher and the 408, where he clearly indicated his name. I believe the 340 Cipher is still considered one of the most sophisticated ciphers in history. It is nothing but rubbish. It is my father's complete name, "Earl Van Best Jr.," spelled out backward. He did it that way to indicate to Avery and anybody else who wanted to take a stab at cracking that puzzle. He put a big backward "B" right in the column that would be the beginning of his last name, "BEST." I think he made that "B" backward to indicate to somebody who was fairly sharp that he was going to put his name backward in that cipher.

After he realized no one was going to crack this cipher, he wrote one last cipher and said, "By the way, have you cracked my latest cipher I sent you? My name is ——?" And he put 13 meaningless symbols and 13 letters in — earlvanbestjr. He spelled his name the way he spelled his name, all three ways clearly and completely, perfectly, not adding a space, not adding a symbol, perfectly in the *San Francisco Chronicle*.

You can't take any other suspect and find their name in those ciphers, in that exact order, without adding letters or adding numbers, adding spaces, or taking away symbols. That's one very compelling thing because his ego was such that "You knew who I was back then, and now I know who you are, and you don't remember me." I believe he was threatening to get caught.

Q. What is the second piece of evidence?

A. The other piece of evidence is, as far as I know, the fact that there were only one set of fingerprints left on Paul Stine's cab. It was a clear fingerprint from their suspect. It had to be because it was smeared in blood. The witnesses saw him wiping down the cab. He had always claimed to have never left fingerprints, but there was a pair of leather gloves that fit my father's hand size in that cab. If you recall, the Zodiac tore a piece of Stine's bloody shirt and took it with him. He later mailed pieces back to the SFPD and Paul Avery, as proof he committed the murder.

I can imagine wearing leather gloves, trying to tear something with a slippery substance like blood on a shirt. You're just not going to do it. I believe he took his gloves off, tore the shirt, tried to wipe the cab down, but inadvertently left his fingerprints and his gloves in that cab.

There's one thing very distinguishable about that fingerprint. On his right index finger, there is a clear scar. I have the fingerprints from my father's booking sheet for the statutory rape of my mother. He had a clear scar the same size and the same angle as the scar on the Zodiac Killer's right index finger. I had an independent fingerprint expert validate that.

For me, those two pieces of forensic evidence, in addition to the mountains of the circumstantial evidence that I presented to the San Francisco Police Department, leave no doubt in my mind.

Listen to the full interview with Gary on my website:

https://www.alanrwarren.com/hom-podcast-episodes/episode/8f60b4c6/most-dangerous-animal-of-all-zodiac-killer-gary-lstewart

---

1. Zodiac Killer — Wikipedia. https://en.wikipedia.org/wiki/Michael_Mageau
2. Earl Van Best Jr. — Van Best made San Francisco news in the early '60s when at the age of 28, he began a predatory relationship with a 14-year-old girl. Shortly after meeting Judy Chandler at an ice cream parlor, he married her.

(Who Is Gary L Stewart From Most Dangerous Animal Of All. https://www.refinery29.com/en-us/2020/03/9511445/who-is-gary-l-stewart-most-dangerous-animal-of-all-hulu) She was pregnant with their son, Gary Stewart, at 15. By that time, Van Best had been imprisoned for statutory rape. Van Best, who would go on to be charged with DUIs, fraud, rape, and pedophilia, among other crimes, died in 1984 in Mexico. (There's almost no evidence Earl Van Best Jr. was the .... https://www.sfgate.com/crime/article/Zodiac-Killer-Earl-Van-Best-Gary-Stewart-fx-show-15105150.php)

3. Paul Avery — an American journalist, best known for his reporting on the serial killer known as the Zodiac, and later for his work on the Patricia Hearst kidnapping. Avery joined the *San Francisco Chronicle* in 1959. In the second half of the 1960s, Avery took a leave of absence from the *Chronicle* and moved his family to Vietnam. In Saigon, Avery co-founded Empire News, a freelance photojournalism organization. He expanded Empire News, opening a branch in Hong Kong, before returning to San Francisco in 1969 after three years in Asia. In the mid-1980s, after working for *The Sacramento Bee* and writing a book about the Hearst kidnapping, he signed up with the then Hearst-owned *San Francisco Examiner*, where he stayed until his retirement in August 1994. Avery reported on the Zodiac case, a series of killings—unsolved to this day—that began in December 1968 and ostensibly ended with the death of a San Francisco cab driver in October 1969. At the time, Avery was a police reporter for the *San Francisco Chronicle*. (Paul Avery — Wikipedia. https://en.wikipedia.org/wiki/Paul_Avery) The Zodiac soon wrote Avery (misspelled by the Zodiac as "Averly") a Halloween card, warning, "You are doomed." The front of the card read, "From your secret pal: I feel it in my bones/you ache to know my name/and so I'll clue you in…" Then inside: "But why spoil the game?" Just as

quickly as the threat was made public, a fellow journalist made up hundreds of campaign-style buttons, worn by nearly everyone on the *Chronicle* staff, including Avery, that said, "I Am Not Paul Avery." It was at this time that Avery began carrying a .38 caliber revolver. (Paul Avery — Alchetron, The Free Social Encyclopedia. https://alchetron.com/Paul-Avery)

4. The first communication — On August 1, 1969, three letters prepared by the killer were received at the *Vallejo Times-Herald*, the *San Francisco Chronicle*, and the *San Francisco Examiner*. The nearly identical letters, subsequently described by a psychiatrist to have been written by "someone you would expect to be brooding and isolated," took credit for the shootings at Lake Herman Road and Blue Rock Springs. Each letter also included one-third of a 408-symbol cryptogram, which the killer claimed contained his identity. The killer demanded they be printed on each paper's front page, or he would "cruse (sic) around all weekend killing lone people in the night then move on to kill again until I end up with a dozen people over the weekend." (Unsolved Mysteries of the World: The Zodiac Killer. https://mysteries-blog.blogspot.com/2010/08/zodiac-killer.html)

The *San Francisco Chronicle* published its third of the cryptogram on page four of the next day's edition. An article printed alongside the code quoted Vallejo Police Chief Jack E. Stiltz saying, "We're not satisfied that the letter was written by the murderer" and requested the writer send a second letter with more facts to prove his identity. The threatened murders did not happen, and all three parts were eventually published.

On August 7, 1969, another letter was received at the *San Francisco Examiner* with the salutation "Dear Editor, This is the Zodiac speaking." This was the first time the killer had used this name for identification. The letter was a response to Chief Stiltz's request for more details that would prove he had killed Faraday, Jensen, and Ferrin. In it, the Zodiac included details about the murders which had not yet been released to the public, as well as a message to the police that when they cracked his code, "they will have me."

On August 8, 1969, Donald and Bettye Harden of Salinas, California, cracked the 408-symbol cryptogram. It contained a misspelled message in which the killer seemed to reference "The Most Dangerous Game." He also said he was collecting slaves for the afterlife. No name appears in the decoded text, and the killer said that he would not give away his identity because it would slow down or stop his slave collection. (The Zodiac Killer | Crime Scene ... — Crime Scene Database. http://crimescenedb.com/the-zodiac-killer/)

Unabomber

INTERVIEW WITH DR. MARK G. HEWITT

Ted Kaczynski, a.k.a. the Unabomber, was investigated in 1996 for possible connection to the Zodiac Killer. Kaczynski worked in California at the time of the Zodiac murders, and like the Zodiac, had an interest in ciphers and threatened the press into publishing his communications. However, Kaczynski was ruled out by both the FBI and San Francisco Police Department based on fingerprint analysis, handwriting comparison, and by his absence from California on certain dates of known Zodiac activity.

At this point, it was considered best to go and talk with Dr. Mark G. Hewitt about this theory. Dr.

Hewitt, who has earned a B.A. in Theology, an M.Div. in Ministry, and an MBA and a DBA in Business Administration, is also a true crime author and award-winning public speaker. He travels the world in his quest for intriguing, unanswered questions and enduring mysteries. Hewitt is the author of the acclaimed Zodiac Serial Killer Series: three books dedicated to telling the complete story of California's most notorious unidentified serial killer: *HUNTED: The Zodiac Murders*, *PROFILED: The Zodiac Examined*, and *EXPOSED: The Zodiac Revealed*.

We interviewed Mark on the show twice, once in 2018 and the second time in 2019.

Q. This is the third book in your Zodiac series titled *Exposed: The Zodiac Killer Revealed*. What was your overall conclusion?

A. Well, the conclusion of the third book is that I could understand the case in no other way than to understand that the attacks and the letters had been carried out by

Theodore Kaczynski, also known as the Unabomber.

As I delved into the Zodiac, I realized that there was a lot of staging going on. That there was a lot of dishonesty in the letters. Surprise, a serial killer can actually be a liar as well. The perpetrator of the Zodiac crimes was a lot more intelligent than he let on. The question for me was, "How intelligent was he, and how much staging was going on?" In other words, what could I tell about the case, what could I reasonably say about the killer based on what he has shown us? Was what he showed us fabricated?

I looked into a number of individuals who had been pointed out by others as being suspects of the Zodiac case. I had wine at a winery with one suspect, corresponded with others, and researched into the background of others. When I came across Ted Kaczynski the Unabomber, I found out that a lot of the public information about the Unabomber, the conventional wisdom on him, was untrue. He was extremely intelligent, proven by the fact that what he showed the public was considerably different than who he was as a real person. So, the more I delved into him and understood him, the more I realized he had a lot of similarities to the Zodiac.

Bit by bit, I was able to make connections between the two and demonstrate for myself, on the basis of literary forensics or forensic linguistics through the use of language that Ted Kaczynski was responsible for the Zodiac crimes.

Q. You said the perception of Ted Kaczynski is different than his true self. How would you say that it's different?

A. Most people's perception of Kaczynski, and I include the media's portrayal, is that of a 52-year-old man who came out of a cabin and was responsible for setting off bombs across the country and writing the *Unabomber Manifesto*. That tends to be as deep as most people get into it. That's understandable because when it was first publicized about the Unabomber's crimes, what first came to light was the *Unabomber Manifesto* and the number of bombs he had set. So, people know the Unabomber as a scholarly person who had put out this sixty-page Manifesto, who was a neo-Luddite, did not believe in technology and worried about the technological dangers of society.

FBI profiler John Douglas published a book following the capture of the Unabomber, saying, "Much of the claims of the Manifesto were simply rationalizations for what he was doing. The truth is that serial killers kill because they enjoy killing." Proof of that was that Ted Kaczynski set bombs for 17 years, a total of 16 bombs, in place or sent through the mail, for the purpose of killing people, without saying a word about technology, of being afraid of the dangers of the future, or the need for environmentalism. None of this came out until 1995 in the publication of the *Unabomber Manifesto*.

Q. Now, his Manifesto came out in '95, but the bombings began in 1978, correct?

A. Yes, that's correct.

Q. So, how do you compare the Zodiac and Unabomber?

A. One of the most fascinating facets in comparing the two that I found is the timeline. The Unabomber, Ted Kaczynski, began bombing in 1978 when he was at the age of 36. When the FBI caught Kaczynski in Montana at his cabin, they were looking for somebody who was approximately 40 years of age.

The idea being that serial killers almost invariably begin their work between the ages of 18 and 25. So, in the mid-nineties, they were looking for a 40-year-old as somebody who had perpetrated all of these bombing attacks for the last 17 years. They were quite surprised to find Kaczynski was 52, almost 53 when he was arrested. The question was, "Why the gap in age?" What do we understand about those 12 years?

The start of the Zodiac murders, which I believe started in Riverside in 1966, when at the time Ted Kaczynski was 24 years of age. In Kaczynski's own words, he went through a very severe emotional and philosophical breakdown in 1966, where he was filled with incredible rage. He decided that he could kill anybody he wanted to. He wanted to have an enemy, and he was looking for people to kill at that time. He was so filled with rage and anger.

We're supposed to believe that he did not act on that rage in 1966 and instead became the Unabomber when he placed his first device in 1978. So, at 36-years old in 1978, he was quite a bit older than when serial killers start to commit murder. But the two killers' timelines match up exceedingly well if you understand that the Zodiac started in 1966 when Ted Kaczynski was entering the last year of his doctoral studies. At the time, he was interviewing in California, looking for a teaching position.

He moved to California to become a professor at Berkley from 1967 to '69. The first canonical Zodiac happened in December of 1968 when Ted Kaczynski was on Christmas break. One month after that attack, Kaczynski submitted his resignation to the school. His final day of being a professor was June 30, 1969, four days after the "Blue Rock Springs Attack" occurred.[1]

Now, if you look at the two years following Kaczynski's time at Berkley, there are kind of a lost two years of his life. It's very difficult to place him anywhere specifically. He wasn't working except for a couple of years over the wintertime. But during the two years following his resignation, the following things happened: the Blue Rock Springs attack, the sending of the three-part letters, the sending of the More Material letter, the attack at Lake Berryessa, the murder of Paul Stine, and the sending of approximately a dozen other letters. Almost all of the Zodiac case letters happened, up until 1971, in March, I believe, when the Zodiac wrote to the L.A. Times. That was the last letter where the "Zodiac" name was used and the last authenticated letter where the "crosshairs" was used.

Why is that significant? Because a few months later, in June of 1971, Ted Kaczynski moved to Montana and built his cabin. Following the move to Montana, there's not a single Zodiac letter that's been authenticated that used the word "Zodiac." There are a few considered Zodiac letters, but again they were a different tone and a different style.

Q. You were talking about that period of time from 1969 to '71. We've heard a lot of talks that Ted Kaczynski was in Illinois or that he was looking to buy land in Canada or Montana in those two years. Some people believe that he was doing the same thing that he did during the Unabomber era, where he would surreptitiously disappear and travel to the bay area to mail letters and things like that. What is your take on that?

A. Well, during the specific Zodiac attacks, the only alibi Kaczynski had was his brother's word that he spent the entire Summer of 1969 searching for land in Canada.

Apparently, sometime in '69, the brothers were together. They did spend time together in British Columbia, and they did put in an application to homestead on a piece of property owned by the Canadian government. That was eventually denied. But the specific dates of all that has not been made available, and David Kaczynski's word had come into question of when exactly he was there.

Following his time at Berkley, Ted Kaczynski used his parent's address in Lombard, Illinois as his home address. That led some people to believe he had moved to Illinois and stayed there. That was not the case because his mother reported his frequent disappearances or his frequently leaving without so much as saying goodbye or letting them know that he was going to be leaving. He would be gone for a while and then show back up again.

He also sent a letter from Minnesota during that time and showed evidence that he traveled and been in Minnesota. Exactly where he was during those two years is not very clear.

Q. There are two points that we discussed earlier. One of them is what Ted's mother said about him disappearing without any notice. During his Unabomber time, he used to ride a bus for a long stretch to a distant place to mail a letter or get materials and things so that it would be more difficult to trace back to him. The theory was that he might have been doing the same thing during the Zodiac crimes.

Secondly, when you were discussing the Summer of 1969 with his brother, and them supposedly looking for land in Canada, there was some discussion about his brother, David saying Ted had forged a letter from one Berkley professor to another as part of a prank. That took place sometime in the Summer of 1969, which indicates that he was still there at that time.

A. Yes, one suspicion is that Ted and David, following their time in British Columbia, before going back to Lombard, Illinois, or Montana, actually drove to the bay area and spent some time there and then went back to Illinois.

One piece of evidence is that David said in August of 1969 he did some camping in Nebraska with his brother. Going from British Columbia to Illinois, the most direct route is not through Nebraska. It would make more sense if the brothers had gone down through the Bay area first and then driven across interstate 80 to get back to Lombard, Illinois.

Another is that at the time, Ted Kaczynski had a library of approximately 200 books. And at some point, those 200 books made the trip from Berkley up to Montana. It's not clear exactly when and how that happened, whether they were mailed or brought up. But for that summer, supposedly, David met Ted further west, and together they went to British Columbia.

The question is, did the brothers drive back to Berkley, spend some time in the Bay area, and then pick up Ted's books and his other possessions and take them back east. If that's the case, it will put Ted Kaczynski in the area and enable him to send the three-part letters at the end of July and the More Material letter a few days later.

Many people have pointed to those particular letters as disqualifying Ted from being responsible for the Zodiac crimes.

Q. It all comes down to whether Ted Kaczynski had an alibi for any of the Zodiac crimes or the mailings of the Zodiac letters. As far as I know, there's never been any definitive word one way or the other to prove where he was in any of these times. Is that correct?

A. That is correct, yes.

Q. Ted Kaczynski went to great lengths trying not to leave a trail to lead authorities back to him. One of the ways he did that was by taking long bus rides to libraries in other areas, where he would not only mail letters, but there are stories about him going into public restrooms and finding hairs on the floor that he put in a bomb to throw off authorities. So, Kaczynski was cognitive of the fact that he needed to go to great lengths to avoid leaving trails. One of the things you mentioned to me in a previous conversation was about the first bomb he set and what he did to throw off the trail, and how it made it seem like he was somewhere else at the time. Would you like to expand on that?

A. Absolutely. That's an important point that you bring up that Ted Kaczynski was incredibly sophisticated. He put false bottoms on his shoes so that when he walked around and left footprints, the footprints were smaller than the size of his foot. He wore disguises, and he had clothes he wore only for his attacks. He grew a beard and mustache and then would trim it back or cut it back so that he only had a mustache and shorter hair. He would go and commit an attack and retreat to Montana to hide from everybody until his beard and mustache grew back, or his hair grew back so that people didn't associate him with having shorter hair. That's the way that he was spotted in Sacramento when a composite picture was made of him. It showed a man with shorter hair and a very trimmed mustache, which would look very different from how Kaczynski did.

People have said that the Zodiac was smart, but he wasn't as smart as Ted Kaczynski. Ted Kaczynski was a genius. But then you have to say that Ted Kaczynski got caught as the Unabomber, whereas the Zodiac Killer has yet to be identified. So, who is the smarter of the two?

For the first Unabomber device, Ted lived in Montana and let his family know that he was going to Illinois to spend some time with them. He called them when he got to Illinois, and in the phone call, he was still in Montana, or he was not in Illinois. He led them to believe he was somewhere else. Then he planted the first bomb in Illinois and then sometime later showed up at his family home. So, if the family was ever asked, "When did Ted get here? When did he leave Montana," he had the perfect alibi for not having planted this first bomb.

He was very criminally sophisticated as far as trying not to get caught. In fact, he was called "The Junkyard Bomber" by the FBI when they first started to investigate him because all of the items he used in the creation of his bomb were gathered from what could have been in a junkyard. He used batteries and ripped off the covers so they could not be traced back to the manufacturer or to a particular store that stored them. The wired he used, he took them from scraps of something he had found, and the FBI could not trace any of the materials back to him.

That's a great story you mentioned about him going to the Missoula, Montana bus depot, and the bathroom there and finding a black hair on the floor. He took the black hair and cut it into two pieces, putting one in the fold of some duct tape in one of his bombs and the other in a fold of duct tape of another bomb. He was hoping that the FBI would find this hair and start looking for a black-haired person that had different DNA than his. We only know this because of his writings and journals. The FBI never did find those hairs as they were blown up in the explosions, or the FBI just didn't find them. That's the level that Kaczynski would go to prevent capture.

It seems like many of the same strategies Kaczynski used to prevent capture were ones that the Zodiac used as well. The Zodiac claimed to have worn a disguise. He claimed to have only looked that way when he made his attacks. But at other times looked completely different. Zodiac may have had particular clothing that he used on his attacks and used it no other time. The Zodiac was known to get rid of any weapon and never use it again for a different attack. It was always a new weapon. He changed his MO. He didn't leave anything behind that could be traced to him. All the fingerprints collected in the case and all the various items have never been traced to anyone. So, the Zodiac has yet to be identified.

Q. You mentioned Kaczynski's journals. Most people might not know this, but Kaczynski kept meticulous journals of his crimes, but most of them were enciphered. They were in code. It took the FBI some time to crack those codes and find out what was in there. In one of those journals, there were categories Kaczynski created for a certain material or certain content. One category was "Embarrassing," as he wrote, I guess things he thought would make him look bad if people found out about them. Another category was called "Bad Public Relations," which I'm not sure what that would be. I find it hard to believe that there could be anything about Kaczynski that would be considered good public relations in that regard. Then he also mentioned, "Past the Statute of Limitations." Of course, that means with certain crimes, there's a statute of limitations, and if you identify the perpetrator after that statute has expired, you cannot prosecute that person. But as we all know, there is no statute of limitations on murder. So, do you have any opinions on what he was referring to when he said, "Embarrassing" or "Bad Public Relations" or "Past the Statute of Limitations?"

A. I'm not sure how he would categorize different things that he had done. Interestingly, in that document, he listed a number of things by what he needed to do with the evidence. Much of it was for some of the most incriminating evidence he said he had to burn or destroy. That tells us that he was not only cognizant of what was in his possession that could incriminate him, but also his willingness to get rid of something. He was not a hoarder. People have looked to the search of Kaczynski's cabin upon his arrest and said that there was no incriminating evidence of the Zodiac crimes.

While that is true, I would point out that there were categories of items found in the cabin that point to or directly relate to the Zodiac. Found in the cabin were disguises, clothing only used for a particular attack, codes, bomb diagrams, and actually created bombs. Well, all three of these categories relate directly to the Zodiac: codes, disguises, and bombs.

While nothing specific that linked Kaczynski to the Zodiac, such as fingerprints, or DNA, or specific weapons used, or specific disguises used, it's interesting that those same categories are present in the Unabomber's cabin.

If you searched other serial killers like Jeffrey Dahmer, Son of Sam, or BTK, you wouldn't find the same type of material that was found in the Unabomber cabin. That, to me, indicates there is a relationship between the two. There are strong similarities there.

If he were willing to get rid of material that would incriminate him and was concerned about his public relations or about being embarrassed, then we are quite sure that he would not want to be classified as mentally ill or crazy. So, he had every reason to distance himself from his crimes as the Zodiac. He was presenting himself as a scholar who had written a manifesto, which was his reason for attacking. If it came out that he was also the Zodiac, then people would say, "Yes, he is crazy," and "No, the Unabomber Manifesto did not accurately describe his motivation for killing."

Q. It's interesting that you mention him being worried about being perceived as crazy. I think certainly, in most cases, he failed in that regard because that's how most people perceived him. But it's interesting because Ted Bundy was very keen on maintaining his image as a nice guy or an innocent person. Someone once said that it was crazy how he pretended to be innocent in the face of overwhelming evidence of his guilt. And people quite often couldn't understand why he just couldn't admit to the crimes. Someone who knew him once said that it's an odd way of looking at it, but if Ted were to admit that he was a murderer, with mental health problems, and that he was not the person he pretended to be for so long, then it would cast a shadow over every conversation he ever had with anyone. And that he would no longer have a real 'self' anymore. He would be known as this murderer.

Ted Kaczynski obviously was not a social creature. He isolated himself and spent a lot of time alone in his cabin. Apparently, he did not like people. I think you mentioned that in his journals, he talked at great length about his desire to kill people. There have been theories that Ted Kaczynski cannot be the Zodiac because he was a bomber and bombers "kill from afar," not "up close and personal." And the Zodiac was obviously an "up close and personal" killer, who shot people and stabbed them. He confronted his victims face to face. But there are stories about Ted Kaczynski that have surfaced over the years. Such as the time he waited inside a car with a knife for a female coworker. Apparently, he was planning to attack that person. He changed his mind, or something happened. There are stories about him stabbing dogs in the woods around his cabin and shooting at airplanes. There's even a theory that some people think he was responsible for the shooting of a worker who was out doing some sort of work in the wooded area around his cabin.

So, what do you think about the criticisms of the theory that Kaczynski is the Zodiac? Do you know about those incidents I described or any others that I may have missed?

A. Everything you mentioned did actually happen and have been attributed to Ted Kaczynski, either from writings in his journal, eyewitnesses, or the evidence in the case. I find it really curious when people's knee-jerk reaction is that Ted Kaczynski couldn't be the Zodiac because he killed from afar with bombs, and the Zodiac killed up close and personal. That demonstrates somebody who doesn't know a whole lot about the Zodiac case. The more you get into the case, the more you realize that the Zodiac changed his MO from attack to attack. That is not uncommon, but the rate and magnitude of change the Zodiac experienced with each attack was actually quite notable. He used different weapons and different types of weapons: he used a tiny blade, he used a butcher knife, he used a .22 caliber weapon, and he used a 9 mm weapon.

Q. In the first two Zodiac attacks, he just walked right up and shot people, whereas, in the third and fourth attacks, he talked to the victims and interacted with them. Especially with the people at Lake Berryessa, where he carried on a conversation with them for a period of time and lied to them about his intent, saying, "I just want to rob you." Then obviously, with the murder of cab driver Paul Stine, he had to interact with that person on some sort of social level when he first got in the cab until they got to the crime scene.

A. Correct. So, in my book, *Profiled*, I make the observation that one of the MOs of the Zodiac Killer was that he changed his MO. He changed it dramatically, and he changed it often. So, to say that the Zodiac couldn't become the Unabomber is kind of strange in that light.

Following the Zodiac sighting when he killed Paul Stine, he stopped killing. He stopped killing and became a letter writer. John Douglas, the FBI profiler, said that the Zodiac was probably very scared, and so he stopped killing up close. What did he do? He started writing letters. And in the subsequent letters, he included two bomb diagrams. Well, bomb diagrams suggest killing from afar using bombs. So, the Zodiac himself changed from somebody who killed up close and personal to somebody who didn't kill, as far as we know, and began to send bomb diagrams through the mail threatening to kill from afar. To say the Zodiac couldn't become the Unabomber is like saying the Zodiac couldn't become the letter-writing Zodiac.

Q. Although the Zodiac did send several bomb diagrams, there's no evidence that he ever actually planted any bombs or any of the bombs that he claimed to have built were ever used or exploded to the best of our knowledge.

A. That is correct. But then I would add that somebody who was obsessive-compulsive like the Zodiac, who threatened to send bombs through the mail, and throughout a couple of years with the letters, society began to ignore him because the bombs were not real. He could not prove that there were bombs. It's conceivable that he obsessively began to think about bombs and then became a bomber because he originally made those threats.

Otherwise, you have to ask how this math professor, who quit his job in 1969, became a bomber in 1978. What's the connection? People know the Unabomber and identify Ted Kaczynski as that Unabomber. But the question is how a math professor morphed from being an expert and genius in math to becoming more interested in chemistry and physics, the fields required for building bombs.

Q. The Zodiac first started by, immediately after the murder of Paul Stine, mocking the police for not catching him and saying that schoolchildren make nice targets. He talked about shooting kids as they got off of the school bus. Of course, that created quite a stir, and the police called him a sloppy criminal who left fingerprints and had been seen by witnesses. He responded with a letter where he said, "I'm not going to tell you when I kill people anymore. I'm going to make my murders look like routine robberies or fake accidents or killings of anger." He also said that he had grown angry with how the police were treating him and telling lies about him, and he was going to take his ball and go home. It was after that that the bomb threats started coming. Unfortunately, for the Zodiac, and if it was Ted Kaczynski, that also coincided with the time when the authorities began to question the wisdom of publishing everything that he was saying, especially his bomb threats. The peak of the time, the Zodiac was trying to use these bomb threats was also, as you said, during a time when people weren't as impressed with or afraid of him anymore. When the media and the police were suppressing most of his threats, might it have contributed to why he, as you said, became obsessed about making these bombs and using them?

A. Exactly. That traces the situation very well.

Q. You have laid out some of the points that you think makes Kaczynski the Zodiac suspect. I'm just going to list the items, and if you like, you can comment on them for the listeners:

- There are mathematical elements to the Zodiac letters which correspond to Ted Kaczynski,

- There's the bomb connection,

- The Zodiac's messages were similar to the Unabomber's,

- The words used by the Zodiac and Unabomber were similar in some instances,

- The categories of content such as the codes and disguises found in his cabin, and

— The connection, or possible influence or inspiration of Joseph Conrad's novel, *The Secret Agent*.

A. Yes, those are the six clusters of evidence that I found that connect Ted Kaczynski to the Zodiac. In exploring Ted Kaczynski, I found these large clusters of evidence that pointed out Kaczynski was probably responsible. One of them you mentioned was mathematics. If you familiarize yourself with the letters of the Zodiac, you find out very quickly that there are a lot of numbers and a lot of symbols. There's a lot of vocabulary and phrasing that is reminiscent of a math professor's equation. Even the Zodiac's crosshair symbol is not the symbol of a gun sight, which is how it was interpreted when it was first received. The Zodiac, in subsequent letters, used these crosshairs symbols in different ways. He made marks around the circle, and he put numbers around another crosshair symbol.

Why was he using these in a strange way? It was because the crosshairs symbol is a mathematical symbol that is a visual demonstration of the equation $x^2 + y^2 = 1$. Why was that significant? It's so basic in mathematics that it has its own term called a unit circle, and it's used extensively. It was used in Ted Kaczynski's particular branch of mathematics. Two of his published papers used the phrase a crosshair circle or a unit circle in the very first sentence. That was how significant it was.

As I got to know the Zodiac letters, I realized this person has a connection to numbers and manipulating numbers in mathematics. The word radiance in the Zodiac letters, and it's used twice, is a very unusual word. It's a word that comes from mathematics, and it's used extensively in mathematics. In Ted Kaczynski's library that was taken out of the cabin, not only were there mathematics books that made use of the word radiance, but Kaczynski wrote in his own handwriting "radiance" in the margin of two of his books.

So, that was one of the clusters. There was a mathematical basis to the Zodiac. In fact, the coding itself is a mathematical activity. You look at all of the symbols the Zodiac used in his codes, and they all came from mathematics. They are used extensively in mathematical papers and mathematical descriptions and equations.

There was a book published in 1907, *The Secret Agent*, by Joseph Conrad, a Russian born, Polish person who lived in England. That particular book is more than a short story, but less than a novel, maybe 50 – 70 pages long. It was a very favorite book of Ted Kaczynski when he was growing up. At one point, when he was having problems with his family, he asked his family members to read *The Secret Agent* and take special note of the professor because Kaczynski told his family, "you really need to read this to understand me and my priorities." As I got to know the Zodiac letters, I found a strong connection to the book *The Secret Agent*: the vocabulary, punctuation, grammar, and even sentence structure. It showed that it was quite likely the person who wrote the Zodiac letters had been steeped in Joseph Conrad's novel. Even some of the strange things like the number 37 in one of the letters. People wonder where the number 37 came from. Well, it's present in *The Secret Agent*. So are the numbers 9 and 10, the phrase "Cab of Death," and it goes on and on. In my book, I list pages and pages of similar vocabulary, not only similar, but identical vocabulary, identical phrases, and identical punctuation.

Q. Have you discussed this with the FBI Agent Jim Fitzgerald? He was the one that caught the Unabomber? [2]

A. I've had some contact with him, and he indicated to me that when Ted Kaczynski was arrested, some wanted to investigate him more fully for his responsibility in the Zodiac crimes. But Jim was convinced that it was a different type of killer and that Ted Kaczynski didn't fit the Zodiac profile. So, he told me in kind of a proud manner that "he shut them down, and he did not want them looking into it any further." Take that as you will. Jim Fitzgerald has published a book that says Ted Kaczynski was not responsible for the crimes of the Zodiac. But he also told me personally that it wasn't looked into, and he shut them down because it didn't make sense to him.

Q. There is an effort to find definitive Zodiac DNA, and we don't know for sure that they have any. To the best of my knowledge, Ted Kaczynski's DNA is not available, or at least he has not provided a sample. However, they might have obtained it from items in his cabin or something like that. But there's no official Ted Kaczynski DNA sample that can be accessed, or it's not in a database. Is that correct?

A. That is correct. A few years ago, the FBI indicated they wanted a sample of Ted Kaczynski's DNA because they were investigating him for the Chicago Tylenol Murders. The fact that they requested a sample tells us that they do not have his DNA. If they do have it from letters or whatnot, it was obtained at least 20-years ago using 20-year-old techniques of gathering DNA. It's far more advanced now, and they would like a complete profile. And to my knowledge, they have not collected one.

Q. You have corresponded with Ted Kaczynski. Would you like to comment on the last letter you received from him?

A. I corresponded with him for about two years. A friend of mine asked me why I didn't just write to him and ask him if he was the Zodiac. I didn't think that was the smartest tactic. I decided to correspond with him under the guise that I was interested in his Manifesto and that it moved something within me. And I wanted to take some action but wasn't sure how to do that.

He just ate up everything I said. I told him what I assumed he wanted to hear, and I was absolutely right. So, he sent, I think, about half a dozen letters to me answering my questions about the Manifesto. Throughout our correspondence, I noticed phrases he used that were reminiscent of the Zodiac letters, and I published some of these in my book *Exposed*.

The last letter I received was after a friend of his told him I wrote about him and that I researched the Zodiac case. Well, Kaczynski was very upset with me and wrote a very angry letter. In some way, it reminded me of the Exorcist Letter. I could see a lot of anger and the pressure he put on the pen as he wrote on the paper. The way he was very terse and is not a person who is able to express his anger. What I got from him was as close as it was going to get to verbalizing anger. But he was obviously very angry with me. He wrote the word "Zodiac," which I found quite fascinating because when I lined that up with the Zodiac writing of the word Zodiac, it looks very similar.

Kaczynski never denied that he was the Zodiac. In fact, he slighted me for having an unwholesome interest in a high-profile murderer. He never asked if the only reason I was writing him was because I suspected him of being the Zodiac. He never addressed that. He never brought that up, which I found quite curious because obviously, if I'm writing about and researching the Zodiac, then the only reason I'm writing to him is because of that.

Listen to the full interviews with Mark on my website:

https://www.alanrwarren.com/hom-podcast-episodes/episode/dd5ede54/anne-penn-what-if-golden-state-killer-zodiac-solved

https://www.alanrwarren.com/hom-podcast-episodes/episode/7066b5ab/hunted-the-zodiac-murders-mark-g-hewitt

1. Blue Rock Springs Attack — On July 4th, 1969, shortly before midnight, Darlene Elizabeth Ferrin and Michael Renault Mageau pulled into the parking lot of the Blue Rock Springs Park in Vallejo. According to Mageau, approximately five minutes later, the same brown car, thought to be a Chevrolet Corvair or Ford Mustang, returned, but this time drew up to within 10 feet of the rear of their car, slightly to the right side. The lone driver exited the vehicle carrying what Michael Mageau described as a "high powered flashlight, the type you carry with a handle" and armed a 9 mm semi-automatic handgun as he casually approached the couple's car. Michael Mageau, believing the person to be a policeman because of his demeanor, searched for some personal identification. At which point, the man raised the handgun and, without uttering a word, fired a volley of five rounds at point-blank range through the passenger side window, striking Michael Mageau and Darlene Ferrin several times. (Blue Rock Springs Attack — ZODIAC CIPHERS. https://www.zodiacciphers.com/blue-rock-springs-attack.html)
2. James Fitzgerald — was promoted to Criminal Profiler at the National Center for the Analysis of Violent Crime, which would later become the FBI's Behavioral Analysis Unit, or BAU. Through myriad investigations of homicide, serial rape, extortion, kidnapping, and workplace violence, Fitzgerald refined his skills in forensic linguistics and threat assessment, specialties that were used to discover the Unabomber. (James R. Fitzgerald — Wikipedia. https://en.wikipedia.org/wiki/James_R._Fitzgerald)

George Hodel | The Black Dahlia Killer

INTERVIEW WITH STEVE HODEL

Retired Police Detective Steve Hodel argues in his book *The Black Dahlia Avenger* that his father, George Hodel,[1] was the Black Dahlia killer, whose victims included Elizabeth Short. The book led to the release of previously suppressed files and wire recordings by the Los Angeles District Attorney's office of his father, which showed that the elder Hodel had indeed been a prime suspect in Short's murder.

In a follow-up book, *Most Evil*, Hodel argued a circumstantial case that his father was also the Zodiac Killer based on a police sketch, similarity in the style of the Zodiac letters to the Black

Dahlia Avenger letters, and questioned document examination.[2]

Hodel appeared on the show twice. The first time was in 2015 concerning his father and the Black Dahlia murders, and the second time was in 2016, discussing his book *Most Evil* about his father being the Zodiac Killer.

Q. How did you connect your father to the Zodiac murders?

A. From the conclusion of the Black Dahlia and the L.A. Lone Women murders investigations, from the police reports, I was pulled into the possibility that George Hodel could have reinvented himself as the Zodiac in the sixties and started up the same MO and signatures and stuff. I wouldn't have even gone there except for the police reports on the Elizabeth Short murder actually showing my dad was investigated for some crimes in Chicago. That's what took me down the rabbit hole to write the book *Most Evil*, and now *Most Evil II*.

In *Most Evil*, I made a compelling case that George Hodel was the Zodiac, but I didn't say "case closed." I said, let's do some DNA and look at this. Let's get him ruled in or ruled out on the DNA. Well, we still haven't developed a confirmed DNA. But over the last five years, I continued working on it, and now I am with the latest book *Most Evil II* saying, yes, we have solved the case. I offer my reasons and proof and believe me, my reputation is on the line. I would not come out and say that he was the Zodiac unless I felt that I had absolutely made the case, and that's what I've done in the new book.

Q. What have you found out that's new for the second book?

A. Basically, I'm offering a signed confession by Zodiac in one of the original ciphers. A French man solved one of the ciphers and contacted me about it, and we worked together on it. The cipher decrypted is actually a signed confession of the crimes by George Hodel. I can't believe he would do this, how stupid. But it was one of his weaknesses; his hubris was his ultimate undoing. He was a megalomaniac, and he concealed this in cryptic language that he thought nobody would ever break. My critics are going to have a tough time with this one because there are five letters, HODEL, and I don't know what they're going to be able to do with that? That's only part of it, but it's what I call "The Rosetta Stone."

Q. What about the age of your father during the Zodiac murders?

A. The biggest hurdle that I had for myself was deconstructing myths. One of them being the age of the Zodiac. I first thought there was no way my father could have been the Zodiac because he was a much younger man. Well, guess what, once I got into the weeds of it, I discovered from the original police reports and stuff, that age discrepancy disappeared.

In the original bulletin, they had ages 35 to 45. The most reliable and best witness of all of them was Donald Fouke, who saw him leaving the scene of the San Francisco cabbie murder. He came out and said that Zodiac was more like 45. As an investigator, I would have asked him if he could have been 47, 48, or 49, and he would have said, "yes, he could have been."

George Hodel was actually 60 but could have easily passed for mid-forties or mid to late forties. So, suddenly that makes it possible. As far as the physical, everything else fits. The shoe size is the same, on and on. A couple more composites came out by artists that made him look in his early fifties, and they are almost picture perfect to George Hodel, including the glasses.

Q. What are some of the other things you believe tie your father to the Zodiac?

A. Probably the most compelling evidence is this game playing. When Zodiac sent in maps to the police or the press and said, "It has to do with radiance and inches on the maps," he pretty much instructed them to align the compass to true north. I followed his instructions and came up with the circle and one line going through his killings in the Napa area and Vallejo. Another line of the 60-degree radian goes directly through the killings in the Presidio, the Paul Stine cabbie. Also, directly of over the grave of guess who? Elizabeth Short, the Black Dahlia.

Here's the bottom line regarding the Zodiac. Going into my investigation, we've got the Black Dahlia Avenger, a serial killer in Los Angeles, who was sending notes, taunting the police, and all of that. We're starting with a known serial killer who did all the same things that Zodiac did twenty years later.

In my book, I include a chapter with all of the samples of my father's handwriting. Many of the Zodiac notes have been confirmed by experts. I'm not personally really big on handwriting. I have a problem with it. I think it's too subjective. You can get experts to say, yes, it's him, then other experts who say, no, it's definitely not him. Well, that's not science to me.

Q. Now you have connected your father to other serial killings that happened in between the Black Dahlia and the Zodiac, correct?

A. I believe he committed three crimes that happened in Chicago in the forties before the Black Dahlia murder. They were known as the "Lipstick Murders." This case was supposed to be solved, and the murderer was named William Heirens.[3] But when I look at the police reports, I found out that Elizabeth Short went to Chicago to investigate the murders herself. She actually slept with a number of the newsmen to get information on the crimes.

At the same time she is doing that, my dad was away in China for a year. I think what happened was, I believe she wrote a letter or something, or maybe he came back on leave, I'm not sure. Anyway, it said something to my dad like, "You didn't do the murders in Chicago, did you," jokingly or whatever.

The next thing we know, she starts running in fear of her life, and dad unexpectedly comes back from China, quitting his job over there with the United Nations. Within a month, she was dead.

Now, I believe she found out or discovered something that connected him. But here's the kicker: she's tortured, basically bisected, and taken and posed on this lot. And the street where she's posed is Degnan Street. What's the name of the little girl that was murdered in Chicago? It was Degnan.

The next crime we've got is in Manilla. The woman's body was nude, surgically bisected by a skilled surgeon, posed on a vacant lot eight blocks from my father's house in the Philippines. It became one of the most famous murders dubbed the "Jigsaw Murders."[4] What's the name of the street where the body was posed? It was Zodiac Street.

We also have the Riverside murder in '67 of Cheri Jo Bates, which is Zodiac connected. Then in '68, the murders start in the Bay area. The connections to the map all fit into this twisted insanity that gets into surrealism.

Surrealists believe there is no difference between the dream and the waking state. My dad believed that there was no difference between a dream and an action you do of your own volition. So, you can kill, you can do anything you want. There is no God, and there's nothing to stop you from doing all of this. That was his personal insanity. I present 25 murders that I believe he was responsible for from 1940 to 1970.

Listen to the full interview with Steve on my website:

ZODIAC KILLER: THE INTERVIEWS

https://www.alanrwarren.com/hom-podcast-episodes/episode/73c9d3c9/most-evil-zodiac-killer-steve-hodel-2015

1. Steve believes his father, a prominent doctor in downtown Los Angeles in the 1940s, was a serial killer who preyed on women and got thrills from taunting police and newspaper reporters. Hodel believes his father was part of a sex cult and likely did some of the killings in concert with friends. Some deaths, including that of Elizabeth Short, may have even occurred in the basement of the Sowden House on Franklin Avenue, where Steve spent a portion of his youth. He calls his father's killing spree "The Los Angeles Lone Woman Murders." (Black Dahlia detective's search of Hollywood home reveals .... https://www.pasadenastarnews.com/2014/06/02/black-dahlia-detectives-search-of-hollywood-home-reveals-smell-of-death/)
2. Zodiac Killer — Wikipedia. https://en.wikipedia.org/wiki/Cecelia_Shepard
3. William George Heirens confessed to three murders in 1946: Josephine Ross, Frances Brown, and Suzanne Degnan. Heirens was called the "Lipstick Killer" after a notorious message scrawled in lipstick at a crime scene.
4. The Jigsaw Murders — On May 29, 1967, chopped legs wrapped in newspaper were found inside a garbage can on Malabon Street, Sta. Cruz, a stone's throw away from the

Pagoda Soda Fountain. A day later, a headless and legless torso was found on a vacant lot along Epifanio De Los Santos Avenue near the Guadalupe Bridge. It took time for the police to identify the body using the fingerprints of the dead hands, which were subsequently found to match Lucila Lalu y Tolentino. Until now, the head (or skull) has never been found. But an autopsy revealed that she was one-month pregnant at the time of her death. In a desperate search for her head and for her murderer, the police had to dig into her past. It brought up the issues about her common-law husband, Patrolman Aniano Vera, and her lover, Florante Relos, 19, plus two other lovers. From what was left of Lucila, they surmised the murder could only have been committed by someone familiar with the use of knives, such as a butcher, surgeon, or at least a pre-med student. The killer must have used a private vehicle to dispose of the torso and legs, and because these were very cold to the touch when found, the remains, the police said, must have been stored in a freezer. (Lucila Lalu Case – Prime Crime. https://primecrime.home.blog/2019/10/26/lucila-lalu-case/)

Edward Wayne Edwards
INTERVIEW WITH JOHN A. CAMERON

Convicted serial killer Edward Wayne Edwards, who committed five murders between 1977 and 1996, was linked to the Zodiac murders and several other unsolved cases by former Cold-Case Detective John A. Cameron. Cameron's theories were met with "almost universal disdain, especially from law enforcement."[1]

In 2009, Edwards was arrested for murder in Louisville, Kentucky. In 2010, he pleaded guilty to the murders of Billy Lavaco, 21, Judith Straub, 18, Tim Hack, 19, and Kelly Drew, 19. Soon after, in a jailhouse interview, Edwards confessed to killing Dannie Law Gloeckner, 25. In 2011, he was sentenced to death for that killing.

The first murders for which Edwards was convicted, Billy Lavaco and Judy Straub, took place in Ohio in 1977. He received life sentences for these crimes in 2010. The second pair of murders, another double homicide, occurred in Concord, Wisconsin, in 1980 when Tim Hack and Kelly Drew were stabbed and strangled. This were referred to as the "Sweetheart Murders." Edwards was questioned at the time, but there was no basis to hold him. Almost 29 years later, his connection to the crime was established through DNA testing. Edwards's daughter, April Balascio, tipped off police about his possible involvement.

Edwards confessed to the 1996 murder of 25-year-old Dannie Boy Edwards in Burton, Ohio. The victim had lived with Edwards and his family for several years as an unofficially adopted son. Dannie's original name was Dannie Law Gloeckner. Edwards murdered Gloeckner in a scheme to collect insurance money. Edwards was sentenced to death for this crime in March 2011.

According to Phil Stanford in his book *The Peyton-Allan Files*, Edwards may have been responsible for the murders of Beverly Allan and Larry Peyton in Portland, Oregon, in 1960. Two men were arrested and imprisoned for these murders but released from prison early. Authorities maintain that the correct persons were prosecuted.

In March 2017, Detective Chad Garcia of the Jefferson County Sheriff's Office, who was in charge of the "Sweetheart Murders" case, described how the murders of Hack and Drew were solved following a tip-off from Edwards's daughter. Garcia said he was "pretty confident" there are at least five to seven more murders Edwards committed, and "who knows beyond that." He gave a list of 15 confirmed and suspected victims, adding that he was less sure Edwards was involved in the Zodiac killings.

Ed Edwards died of natural causes at the Corrections Medical Center in Columbus, Ohio, on April 7, 2011, avoiding execution by lethal injection set for August 31st.[2]

John A. Cameron is a 55-year-old retired Police Detective from Great Falls, Montana. His career in law enforcement began in 1979. He retired in 2005 as a Sergeant of Detectives, working cold cases. He has worked on FBI serial killer task forces, catching ritualistic child cannibal killer Nathan Bar-Jonah. His cases have been featured on *America's Most Wanted, Dateline NBC,* and he helped produce a series known as *Most Evil-True TV.*

We were able to interview Cameron three times over three years, and this is a compilation of the subject of Edwards's being the Zodiac Killer only.

Q. I heard that Edwards would go out and find people to frame for a crime. Is that correct?

A. Firstly, Edwards didn't get caught for any of the murders until he was 76-years old, and he had been killing since he was 11-years old. He was married, and he had five children. He would traipse around the country with his family and force them to change their names and identity. He lived in every part of the country over the decades. And yes, he would target somebody to frame and somebody to kill.

Usually, what he would look for was a cheater. Somebody who was cheating on their wives, or a wife cheating on a husband. Or somebody cheating in another manner, such as financially.

It was kind of based on the "seven deadly sins." If he felt that you had sinned, that gave him the right to frame you. So, he would target individuals, getting to know them years in advance under an assumed identity. Then, he would figure out a plan to kill them and frame somebody close to them. He did that in dozens of murders.

Q. So this was a sort of punishment that he was giving these people who were cheating?

A. That's exactly what it was. Let me just give you an example of the last murder I believe he committed. On May 5th of 2009, two months before he got captured for his first murder, he snuck into the house of a wife, who was sleeping with her two little boys, ages six and 7-years old. The husband had just left the house to go workout in the morning. He strangled the wife and the two little boys. Then he wrote these horrible messages on the wall in red spray paint that said, "You have been punished. I saw you leave. I'm always watching." Things like that. In the messages he wrote on the wall were codes that actually contained the killer's name.

It turned out the husband was cheating on his wife, and he worked for one of the biggest Christian ministries in the world, Joyce Meyer Ministries. He was the head of security. Edwards groomed his way into this man's life for a couple of years, sending him threatening letters saying, "I'm going to get you," or "I'm going to get your kids." And then he did.

That man, Christopher Coleman[3], ended up going down for killing his wife and two kids and has been in prison since 2009. But he is soon to get a new trial. My guess is that he won't even have a new trial but just be released. That is how Edwards worked.

Q. A new trial based on this evidence?

A. Well, Chris Coleman filed an appeal on the basis of Ed Edwards. Then a lawyer got in touch with him, and they decided to file another appeal in a separate court, based on some other information they had uncovered in a court record. That really is the most important in an appeal -that you have to rely on what was played out in court. It turns out they found some exculpatory evidence that was withheld from them.

Q. You get a lot of flack from people because you seem to place a lot of murders on Ed Edwards. This must open up old wounds for the families who already thought their case was solved.

A. Yeah, but you also have the family members of the person who was wrongly convicted for a murder now sitting on death row. The fact is that Edwards's crimes, his murders, were always designed to steer the evidence to someone innocent so that he could frame somebody. Those convictions were just wrong, and it's very difficult to get them overturned. But, just in the last few years, several of those cases have been overturned that Ed had been involved in.

Q. Was Edwards putting himself in the position of God? Saying things like, "I know your sin," "I'm watching," "I'm God," "I'm going to punish you for this," "You ought to suffer for your crime."

A. That is how he really saw himself. One thing you have to realize is that Edwards was the Zodiac Killer.

When you read his letters, he said he was collecting slaves for the afterlife. So he could rule them in their afterlife. And what that portrays is Satan. He'd pick people who were cheating and sinning, and in his mind, they were going to go to hell. So he was going to punish them by killing someone they knew and then frame them for the murder.

That's why a lot of the Zodiac cryptograms were based on ancient Egyptian history, where these ancient evil men were considered Gods. And Gods ruled the dynasties. That's what he considered himself to be. He was in control of all things. That's what he wrote in the Zodiac letter of 1977. What he meant in the letter was control of the media, the cops, the courts, etc. He was God.

Q. Why do you think he wore a mask during some murders, then not in others?

A. In his 1972 autobiography, *The Metamorphosis of a Criminal: The True-Life Story of Ed Edwards,* he talked about how he didn't like to wear a mask. He wanted people to see him so he could be identified. What he would do is subtly change his appearance with very professional Hollywood-style make-up. He would change the bridge of his nose, or the length of his ears, using reconstructive putty to make people look different in movies.

But the reason for wearing the Zodiac executioner's hood in 1969 in Lake Berryessa and leaving one person alive was to create terror. Because that picture of the

Zodiac wearing that hood, and what he did to that couple at Lake Berryessa, is scary.

Then, he sent the letter stating he was collecting slaves for the afterlife. He purposely left the man alive in 1969, so he could describe him. He actually detailed who he was to that man and connected him to Deer Lodge Prison, Montana, where I was working when I was introduced to Edwards. Edwards had been in Deer Lodge Prison 13 years before the Zodiac murders.

Q. So Edwards was behind writing the letters to the press as the Zodiac Killer?

A. Yes, he did that his whole life. He taunted the press and different police organizations with letters like that. The last letter I was able to find that the Zodiac wrote was on June 14, 2008, when a pregnant woman was killed in a bathtub in Fort Bragg. Edwards wrote the Zodiac sign in lipstick on the mirror, and then he sent a letter saying, "I was at the scene watching the Fayetteville police and how stupid they were."[4]

Before 2008, there were Zodiac letters for decades, and everybody questioned if they were real or copycat. The fact is, Edwards never got caught until he was 76-years old, and he was always sending letters.

Q. So, why use a cipher on some and not others?

A. In all the letters he sent, there were always clues to his name, and sometimes he would use numbers written within the letters. Those numbers would be 5 and 4, or 4 and 5, or 5 and 5. Those numbers in the alphabet are E and D, or E and E, so it was always Ed, or Ed Edwards was the killer.

That's what he did in his last killing in 2009-he put the numbers 4 and 5 and the name Ed right on the wall. It made no sense to anybody looking at it, especially a police officer at such a horrible scene. They wouldn't have known what was going on until you knew that this was the work of the Zodiac Killer.

Q. Did you get any letters from Edwards?

A. I got letters from Edwards for almost a year, and he always included cryptograms in my letters. I knew he was the Zodiac, but he kept telling me that it's so much worse than you think, John. I frame people. I didn't understand it at the beginning. He was never going to stand up and say that he was the Zodiac Killer because that's not what he wanted. What the Zodiac wanted was to kill in his afterlife. And how he did that was to frame people. Some are on death row, and that's how he's still killing in his afterlife.

Q. Why all the grandiosity?

A. Grandiosity was for recognition, and that's what he called it throughout his life. He was into crying for recognition. What it really meant was that he was into murder for recognition. His murders would be recognized; they would go on for decades. They would be talked about. There would be movies about him, and there would be books about him. He could sit home any day, read the paper, and say, "That's mine." In his head, he didn't need the public to say that he was the Zodiac. He didn't want that. He wanted to keep them guessing, even after his death, so that it would play out like this for decades.

Q. When you were on the show the first time, you believed that Ed Edwards was behind the murder of Teresa Halbach, who was brought to fame from the Netflix Miniseries, *Making a Murderer*. Do you still believe that to be true?[5]

A. Yes, very strongly. That whole case just had the fingerprints of the Zodiac and Ed Edwards. It really was the ritualistic nature of that murder occurring on Halloween and targeting a man named Avery. Avery, of course, was a huge name in the Zodiac case. The San Francisco reporter Paul Avery was taunted by the Zodiac with a Halloween card saying, "Ha Ha. I'm going to leave you a clue in this card." There was actually a skeleton's hand with Ed Edward's date of birth, 6, 14, of 33 on the card. That was the clue, but you had to know who Ed

Edwards was, and you had to know his date of birth in order to see it. It's clear as day in that card.

Q. In the documentary that you are making about Edwards, you have one of his grandsons working with you. Does the family believe he was the Zodiac Killer?

A. Ed Edwards has been married three times. When he was caught, he was married to that wife for 43 years, and he had five children with her. Two of the children participated in the documentary we did. They are convinced that their father was the Zodiac. He forced them to sit down and watch Zodiac movies when they were children. When it didn't play out the way he knew it did, he would scream at the television, "That's not how it happened."

They feel very sure that he was the Zodiac and that he also killed Jimmy Hoffa.[6] Those are the two things they are certain of. The rest of it, they're skeptical.

Q. How did Hoffa get into this? Did Edwards want to punish him for his behavior as well?

A. Jimmy Hoffa and Ed Edwards went to prison together in 1967. In Leavenworth Prison, they served time together for a year, year, and a half. Jimmy Hoffa promised Ed Edwards a job when he got out on parole in 1967 with a trucking firm with the Teamsters. When Ed got out, Hoffa failed him and didn't come through. Hoffa also called Edwards a homosexual, and that's what really ticked off Ed. Then, in 1975, Jimmy Hoffa was pardoned by Richard Nixon. That really ticked off Ed because he earned his parole, and here was Jimmy Hoffa getting a pardon from the President of the United States.

So, he decided to create a crime of recognition, something that would go down in history, that we would all laugh about on late-night talk shows, "Where is Jimmy Hoffa?" His body will never be found because Edwards knew how to blow up bodies into little bits, just like he did to

Teresa Halbach. Jimmy Hoffa is detailed in his book. There's a couple of pages about him. In fact, Edwards was the informant in the Hoffa case that steered the evidence to a couple of gangsters out of Detroit.

Q. Will they ever be able to convict Edwards of the Zodiac murders? Or any of the other famous cases, such as Jimmy Hoffa?

A. They will never convict him or investigate him now that he's dead. But what's happening is many defense attorneys are investigating the cases. They now have innocent people in jail, and that will be exposed. I believe the one that will expose it the most is the Christopher Coleman case from May 5, 2009. Where the two little boys and the wife were strangled in bed, that one will be thrown out, and then all will be exposed. Law enforcement won't do it.

Q. Was Edwards ever a suspect at the time of any of the murders you believe that he did?

A. Yes, the one in 1980, the "Lovers' Lane" murder in Wisconsin. He was the suspect right at the beginning because he was seen with a bloody nose. He worked in the place where the couple was killed. He fled the county within days of it happening. Then went off the radar. They didn't know who he was. About 30 years later, his daughter turned him in.

Q. What actual forensic or physical evidence do you have connecting Edwards to any of these murders?

A. Like the Zodiac Killer, it was always about the writings: the letters he was going to send, the book he ended up writing, the TV appearance. He threw it in our faces in the letters, but you had to know his name, Edward Edwards, in order to put the puzzle together. That's what the Zodiac was possibly doing when sending in cryptograms and everything saying, "Come on, catch me if you can." That's how the whole thing tied together, through his writings.

As for forensics, I begged police departments to retest and do other things, and they didn't then. But now they are. All of a sudden, the Zodiac case is back in the limelight. And they're taking all of those letters and going back to the drawing board with DNA. I really believe that in the future, there will be a case where they will get his DNA, and he will be exposed for who he was-the Zodiac.

Q. Do we have Edwards' DNA on file now?

A. Yes, he's entered into CODIS.[7] But what's happening now is they're checking other databases. People are submitting their own DNA to genealogy sites, and they're going to be able to get a lot of hits. Edwards planted a lot of the DNA at the scenes. In some of the scenes, he planted hair, fibers, blood, semen, and urine. I know that he also planted other victim's DNA at murders he committed later. He would leave noticeable hairs clutched in the hands of people. Those hairs were considered to be the killer's, but they weren't. They were actually another victim of the killer.

Listen to the full interviews with John on my website:

https://www.alanrwarren.com/hom-podcast-episodes/episode/b3d0876f/edward-wayne-edwards-john-cameron

https://www.alanrwarren.com/hom-podcast-episodes/episode/b46a72fb/edward-wayne-edwards-john-cameron-encore

1. Zodiac Killer — Wikipedia. https://en.wikipedia.org/wiki/Michael_Mageau
2. Edward Edwards (serial killer) — Wikipedia. https://en.wikipedia.org/wiki/Edward_Wayne_Edwards
3. On May 5, 2009, at 5.43 a.m., Christopher Coleman left his comfortable suburban house in Waterloo, Illinois, to go to the gym. After his workout, he said he called home and was worried when no-one answered. So he rang a neighbor, Police Officer Justin Barlow, to check on his family. At trial, Officer Jason Donjon, who entered the house with Barlow, testified that they found the house covered in threatening messages daubed in red paint. The graffiti read, "I am watching," "punished," and "u have paid."

   Then they discovered the bodies of Mrs. Coleman and her two sons killed in separate bedrooms. Mrs. Coleman was left naked in bed, strangled with a ligature. Her eldest son, Garett, was curled up in bed with spray paint on his sheets. Finally, the youngest, Gavin, was seen lying face down with his limbs dangling either side of the bed and swear words daubed on his covers. (Babylon Prime: Court upholds life sentence for .... https://babylonprime.blogspot.com/2015/03/court-upholds-life-sentence-for.html)

   According to police computer experts, Coleman's laptop, accessed by his own password, was the source of anonymous profane threats against his family that Coleman had reported to police as early as November 2008. Coleman was convicted of the murders in 2011.
4. Sgt. Edgar Patino, 27, was arrested and charged with first-degree murder in the death of Army Spc. Megan Touma, a 23-year-old Fort Bragg soldier found dead in a motel bathtub in Fayetteville, N.C. Patino was married to another woman but confirmed he had fathered Touma's unborn child. He would not comment on a specific motive

or cause of death. Touma died inside a Fairfield Inn motel room either late on June 13 or June 14, 2008.

Fayetteville Police Department received typed letters from someone claiming to be Touma's killer. The letters bore the symbol of San Francisco's famous Zodiac Killer, and a similar symbol reportedly was found inside the motel room where Touma was killed. The letters were dated June 17, but investigators later determined they were both postmarked June 24 and were sent from within Fayetteville. "It was a masterpiece," the letter to the newspaper read, referring to Touma's murder. "I confess that I have killed many times before in several states, but now I will start using my role-model's signature. There will be many more to come." Authorities determined that Patino purchased a typewriter the day before the letters were postmarked. The machine was seized when a search warrant was executed on Patino's home. ('Zodiac' Letters Tied Suspect to GI's Murder-ABC News. https://abcnews.go.com/US/story?id=5479661&page=1)

5. Photographer Teresa Halbach disappeared on October 31, 2005. Her last alleged appointment was a meeting with Steve Avery, at his home on the grounds of Avery's Auto Salvage, to photograph his sister's minivan that he was offering for sale on Autotrader.com. Halbach's vehicle was found partially concealed in the salvage yard, and bloodstains recovered from its interior matched Avery's DNA. Investigators later identified the charred bone fragments found in a burn pit near Avery's home as Halbach's. Avery was arrested for the murder of Teresa Halbach, and in 2007 was convicted and sentenced to life imprisonment without the possibility of parole. In March 2006, Avery's nephew, Brendan Dassey, was charged as an accessory in the Halbach case after he confessed under interrogation to helping his uncle kill Halbach and dispose of her body.

6. James Riddle Hoffa disappeared on July 30, 1975. He was declared dead on July 30, 1982. Hoffa was an American labor union leader who served as the president of the International Brotherhood of Teamsters from 1957 until 1971. Hoffa first faced major criminal investigations in 1957 as a result of the McClellan Committee.

On March 14, 1957, Hoffa was arrested for allegedly trying to bribe an aide to the Select Committee. Hoffa denied the charges and was later acquitted, but the arrest triggered additional investigations and more arrests and indictments over the following weeks. When John F. Kennedy was elected president in 1960, he appointed his younger brother Robert as Attorney General. Robert Kennedy had been frustrated in earlier attempts to convict Hoffa while working as counsel to the McClellan subcommittee.

In May 1963, Hoffa was indicted for jury tampering in Tennessee and charged with the attempted bribery of a grand juror during his 1962 conspiracy trial in Nashville. Hoffa was convicted on March 4, 1964, and subsequently sentenced to eight years in prison and a $10,000 fine. While on bail during his appeal, Hoffa was convicted in a second trial held in Chicago, on July 26, 1964, on one count of conspiracy and three counts of mail and wire fraud for improper use of the Teamsters' pension fund. He was sentenced to five years in prison.

Hoffa spent the next three years unsuccessfully appealing his 1964 convictions. Appeals filed by his chief counsel, St. Louis Defense Attorney Morris Shenker, reached the U.S. Supreme Court. He began serving his aggregate prison sentence of 13 years on March 7, 1967, at the Lewisburg Federal Penitentiary in Pennsylvania.

Hoffa disappeared on July 30, 1975, after he had gone out to the meeting with Provenzano and Giacalone. The meeting was due to take place at 2:00 p.m. at the Machus Red Fox restaurant in Bloomfield Township, a Detroit suburb. The place was known to Hoffa, as it had been the site of the wedding reception of his son James. Hoffa wrote Giacalone's initials and the time and location of the meeting in his office calendar: "TG—2 p.m.—Red Fox." (Jimmy Hoffa — Wikipedia. https://en.wikipedia.org/wiki/Jimmy_Hoffa)

7. CODIS is the acronym for the Combined DNA Index System and is the generic term used to describe the FBI's program of support for criminal justice DNA databases as well as the software used to run these databases. (CODIS and NDIS Fact Sheet — FBI. https://www.fbi.gov/services/laboratory/biometric-analysis/codis/codis-and-ndis-fact-sheet)

Michael O'Hare

INTERVIEW WITH RAY GRANT

True crime author and amateur detective Gareth Penn[1] started writing about the Zodiac case in a 1981 *California Magazine* article entitled "Portrait of the Artist as a Mass Murderer." Penn theorized the Zodiac crime scenes were selected in a way that created a geometric shape over the surface of the San Francisco Bay Area as a "murderous art project." Part of Penn's commentary about his theory included the observation that "other artists had sought to remove their work from the ordinary human perspective. Zodiac trumped them all."

Penn then spent the better part of two decades publicly accusing the University of California,

Berkeley public policy professor, Michael O'Hare, of the Zodiac murders.[2] O'Hare filed an FBI complaint against Penn, and in May 1981, the Bureau investigated him for possible extortion. According to FBI memos, an agent "contacted Penn by telephone and told him that if he was responsible for the correspondence to O'Hare, he should immediately cease and desist, pointing out that it could jeopardize any investigation and he could possibly be subject to both civil and criminal penalties." In a May 1981 meeting with FBI agents, Penn "freely admitted sending material to O'Hare but stated he had no intent to extort anything."[3]

Gareth Penn is close to 80-years old now, and we were unable to find him to see if he wanted to discuss his theories with us on the show. However, another author/researcher named Ray Grant adopted Penn's theories and wrote three of his own books on the Zodiac. Ray has a B.A. in English Writing from the University of Pittsburgh with a minor in psychology. He appeared on the show in 2015.

Q. How do you see the Zodiac Killer?

A. If you read the online Zodiac message boards and websites, you see a lot of psychoanalysis, not just of the Zodiac, but of other people on the various websites. I did an internship at the Western Psychiatric Hospital in Pittsburgh in the early 1970s. I found that people were reluctant to have someone in a clinical environment psychoanalyze them or diagnose them, even with training, a Ph.D., or if you were a psychiatrist.

With phenomena like the Zodiac Killer, people immediately say, "This guy is psychotic. This guy's a psychopath. He's a sociopath." But, unless you have the person in a room somewhere, where you can interview him and get some idea of his background, what he feels, and so forth, trying to psychoanalyze somebody from letters sent or even crimes committed is kind of a wasted effort.

People with a psychological or psychology background like myself are aware of that.

There's this prevalence because the Zodiac Killer is a kind of a "Jack the Ripper." People have latched onto him as this kind of maniac running amok in Northern California with a knife, with blood dripping off it. Somehow that image excited people, largely because the case is unsolved.

Zodiac has become the Jack the Ripper of the late twentieth century and even into the early twenty-first century. You see rumors like Ted Cruz is the Zodiac Killer, which is ridiculous since he was born in 1970, I think. You really have to step back from that and look at the actual evidence in the case. If you're interested in solving it, you use actual criminology and not get sidetracked by psychoanalysis, which can't be done unless you have the person in front of you.

Q. So why did you pick the Zodiac Killer?

A. Around the mid-1970s, I was absolutely fascinated by the "Son of Sam" case. The idea that someone was running around shooting people and then sending letters to the police, just that entire idea, enthralled me. Then I started reading every book on serial killers I could find. That was my initial interest. I was not actually a Zodiac buff. I was more of a serial killer buff. I read every book that came out about Ted Bundy and all the classic serial killers. People like Ed Gein, for example.

What ended up happening was in 1984, I joined the American Mensa, which is a social group for people with IQ scores in the upper two percent of the population. In the July/August 1985 edition of the Mensa Bulletin, there was an article by Gareth Penn, another Mensa member, who wrote an article called, "The Calculus of Evil," which was about the Zodiac case.

Gareth Penn's thesis in that article was that the Zodiac Killer was committing murders to create geometric angles on the landscape. There's a passage in the July 26, 1970 letter, usually called the "Mikado Letter," or the "Little List Letter." There is a postscript where he says, "The Mount

Diablo code concerns radian from the number of inches along the radian."

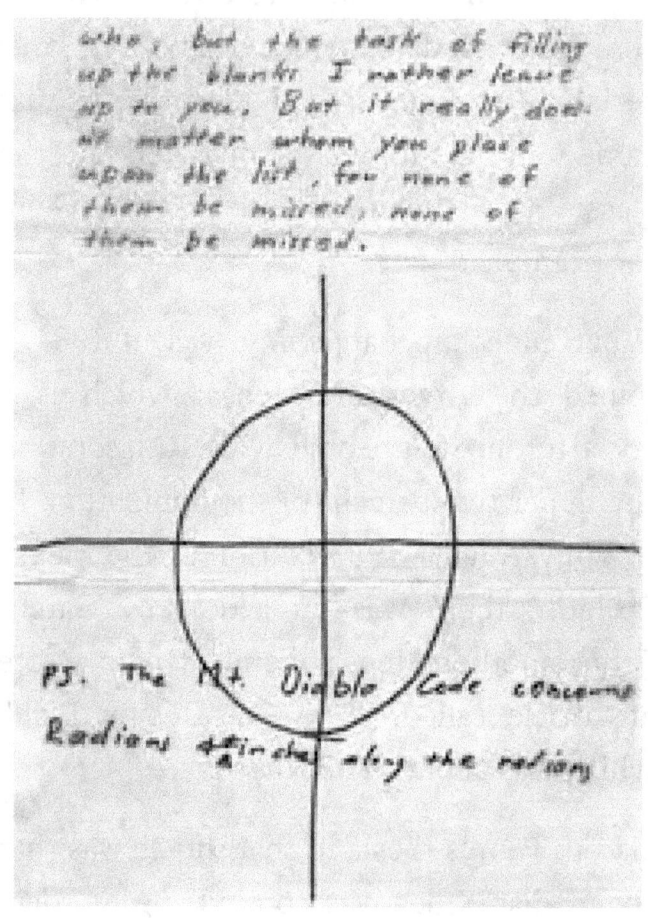

Radian is an angle of 57.29 degrees. If you plot that angle on a map of the San Francisco Bay area, you had an angle which at least approximated 57.29 degrees. In June of 1970, the killer sent a Phillips 66 map that had the peak of Mount Diablo circled. If you connected Mount Diablo to the crime scene at Washington and Cherry, where Paul Stine was murdered, and then made an angle by rotating through the point of Mount Diablo to the murder sites of Lake Herman Road and Blue Springs Park, you ended up with an angle of approximately 57.29 degrees.

Now, if somebody had just observed that and said, "Hey look, it's a Radian," it might not have much merit. But since the writer himself mentioned Radian, the murder sites appeared to be approximately along the lines of a Radian angle, and it seems to me it has to have had some merit.

I began having phone conversations with Gareth and writing to him, and we had extensive correspondence from about July or August of 1985 until May of 1990. During that correspondence, I suspected that Gareth Penn himself might be involved in the Zodiac murders. Gareth named a specific person, who, at the time, was a lecturer at Harvard's John F. Kennedy School of Government, Michael O'Hare.

O'Hare was someone with multiple degrees from Harvard. He was born in New York City in 1943, and he generally resembled the Zodiac sketch, which many people do. Also, his handwriting was very similar to that of the Zodiac Killer. At least the samples I have seen are. Gareth featured them in his book, *Times 17*, which came out in 1987. People who download my book on Amazon, *Zodiac Killer Solved*, can see for themselves. There are samples given there.

But the thing that convinced me most about Michael O'Hare was his article in the March 1967 *Progressive Orchid Picture*, where he created an artificial angle on a model of the MIT Tower. The article was about the difficulty of wind patterns in the vestibule of the Earth Science building at MIT. That's building 54, and externally, it's called the MIT Tower. In creating the illustration for the article, Michael O'Hare created this artificial angle of 117 degrees. Coincidentally, 117 degrees is the longitude of Riverside, California, where the first Zodiac murder took place. That was generally the basis for the suspicion of Michael O'Hare as the Zodiac Killer.

As I said, I began to suspect Gareth's complicity in the Zodiac crimes just based on what he said in his letters. I talk about that in my book. The first 12 chapters are about the conventional evidence in the case, where I analyze the forensics, the ballistics, the circumstantial evidence, and the eyewitness testimonies.

Q. What's your opinion on the conventional evidence in the Zodiac case?

A. Essentially, if you look at the conventional evidence, I believe you will come to the conclusion that the first three victims, Cheri Jo Bates, David Faraday, and Betty Lou Jensen, were all abducted prior to their murder. There's a general pattern in the conventional evidence which leads one to believe the Zodiac Killer was actually multiple people, and that four people were involved in the murders: Michael O'Hare, a lecturer at Harvard, Gareth Penn, the retired librarian, the mother of Michael O'Hare, born in 1907 and died in 1996, and Gareth's father Hugh Penn, born in 1913 and died in 1995, who was a statistician for the California Highway Patrol and the California Department of Justice. The murders were planned and orchestrated, and the evidence backs all of that up.

Q. So what kind of relationship did Gareth Penn have with Michael O'Hare?

A. That's one thing that I can't explain because I have no idea. I can tell you that these four people were involved based on what I know, what they have said, and their own actions. I confronted Michael O'Hare at Harvard in 1990. I wrote a book called *Zodiac Murders Solved*, and I printed out 96 copies. I sent six copies to the Harvard Administration and the other 90 copies to the faculty at the John F. Kennedy school. This would have been in November 1990.

I said that Michael O'Hare was the Zodiac Killer, but if he was innocent of the Zodiac crimes, he had two choices. He could either sue me, take me to court, and so forth. The problem with doing that was if he sued me, I would have the right to ask for his fingerprints. And they could then be compared with the Zodiac prints left at the crime scene from California. People told me that if you sue somebody, you are acknowledging their accusations and that they have merit.

Well, first of all, Michael O'Hare didn't have to sue me to prove he wasn't the Zodiac. He had already talked to the FBI in Massachusetts a couple of times about the Zodiac case after he was initially accused by Gareth Penn. All he had to do was call up the FBI and say, "he had been accused by multiple people of being the Zodiac Killer, and he wanted to submit his fingerprints for comparison with the prints on file at the FBI lab. If he was innocent, that should end the discussion there.

But Michael O'Hare chose not to do that. With my accusation, he chose to immediately quit his job at Harvard, sell his house, and move his wife, who worked for the State of Massachusetts, and his two daughters, who had to leave their friends in the neighborhood. Keep in mind that I was also accusing his mother of the Zodiac crimes. His mother lived in his house, and she had to relocate too. Michael relocated to Berkley, California. If someone accused me of serial murder, I think my first response would be to say that I'm innocent and take whatever you want. If you want my fingerprints, DNA, or what have you, how much more motivated would I be to confront my accuser if that person accused my mother of the same thing. But Michael O'Hare didn't do any of that. He simply absconded to the other end of the country.

Q. What did Harvard say in response to this?

A. There was no upside for Harvard to react one way or the other because if they had a notorious serial killer who was not only a graduate of the school but a member of the faculty, how does it benefit Harvard to admit it? So, they essentially kept quiet about the whole thing.

Q. Did O'Hare contact you personally?

A. No. Michael O'Hare has commented on me in emails that have been forwarded to me. I don't think I can do anything. People are constantly citing an article that Michael O'Hare wrote for the *Washington Monthly* back in the May/June edition of 2009. The name of that article is "Confessions of the Non-Serial Killer."

Essentially, he's talking about his interaction with Gareth Penn. Now, you have to remember that Michael O'Hare was the trigger man in the Zodiac case and the function of Gareth Penn was to be his PR agent. In other words, they had created this interesting puzzle for the world to contemplate. The idea was that after ten years, Gareth would come forward in 1980 and begin to point out this radian angle the killer created.

Michael O'Hare, who looks like the killer, writes just like the killer and seems to have many of the attributes the killer would have, only writes about Penn. He doesn't mention me once. Remember, I'm the person who turned his life upside down. I'm the person who accused him in front of all of his colleagues.

Q. So, how does a Harvard faculty member decide to do the Zodiac killings? And then just stop and go on with his life as normal?

A. Keep in mind that Gareth Penn and I kept up some correspondence for four or five years, and we also talked on the phone many times between 1985 and 1990. I once asked Gareth, "How could someone with Michael O'Hare's background actually kill people?" Because killing people is a tremendous dividing line between us, and the people fascinated with the Ted Bundys and the Dennis Rader, and so forth, we look at them and say I could never do anything like that. Certainly, each one of us, at one point or another, have wanted to kill somebody for various reasons. But we don't do it because we decide that we don't want to end another person's life.

Gareth responded that he was cold-blooded, and you have to remember he's not committing murders for conventional reasons. Ted Bundy committed murders because he had a need, or whatever you want to call it, to murder women. To an extent, you would have to say that he couldn't stop himself-the same thing with Dennis Rader. But in the case of the Zodiac Killer, they weren't doing that because of any psychological need they had. They were doing it because they wanted to create this, whatever you want to call it, this puzzle. I've had my Zodiac work described by people who said, "Well, you think the Zodiac murders were an art project."

They weren't only an art project. Part of the idea was to create a prototypical serial killer who was doing the same things that fascinated me about the Son of Sam. Where not only was he killing people compulsively, but he was writing to the police about it as Dennis Rader did. The

Zodiac Killers were constantly doing that. They were creating this kind of pattern. The Zodiac murders were designed to have a beginning, a middle, and an end. The entire Zodiac project was designed to come to an end on Friday, August 11, 1989, in a specific place in Greater Boston.

The number of times the killer would strike in these public murders was planned out ahead of time. The Zodiac Killer fired ten shots at Lake Herman Road. He fired nine shots at Blue Rock Springs Park. He stabbed a couple at Lake Berryessa. He stabbed the man seven times, and the woman ten times. So, he inflicted 17 stab wounds. Then, at Presidio Heights, he shot Paul Stine once on the right side of his head. So, in other words, he fired 20 shots and inflicted 17 stab wounds. If you remember, the scorecard at the bottom of the Exorcist Letter says, "Me 37 SFPD 0." The 37 is simply the number of times that he struck. So, when people think he means he's had 37 victims, it's not. It means he's struck 37 times, and the SFPD hasn't laid a glove on him.

Q. How did Michael O'Hare choose who the other three people would be to help him commit the Zodiac crimes?

A. I have no idea what the psychological dynamics were for the four people. But what you basically have is the trigger man, Michael O'Hare, the PR man, Gareth Penn, and the other two people were Michael's mother and Gareth's father. What their interaction was, I have no idea.

Q. How did they choose their victims?

A. Well, if you're Hugh Penn (Gareth's father), and statistician for the California Highway Patrol and the Department of Justice, you have access to the state driver database. One of the things we know is that all of the Zodiac crimes were in proximity to a vehicle. For example, when Cheri Bates was murdered, her car was parked about a block west of the murder site, and she was last seen driving her car. The same thing with David Faraday and Betty Lou Jensen. They were found at Faraday's Rambler Station wagon. And Darlene Ferrin was shot in her car. When the two victims were stabbed at Lake Berryessa, the Zodiac walked up to the highway where their car was parked and wrote a note in felt-tip pen on the passenger side door. Paul Stine was shot inside his taxicab. You can locate a victim by tying him to his vehicle. If I have access to the state driver database, that means I know where the person lives. If I have access to the driver's license and registration, I know where the driver lives.

Q. Did the victims know each other or have any connections between them?

A. Yes, there are connections between the victims. For example, the two victims at Lake Berryessa, Bryan Hartnell and Cecelia Sheppard were both Seventh Day Adventists. The Medical Examiner at Riverside, who autopsied Cheri Bates, was also a Seventh Day Adventist. Here's the odd thing: both Cheri Jo Bates and her father, Joseph Bates, had a name that contained the name of the Seventh Day Adventist movement's founder. If you look at the names of the two victims in Vallejo,

David Faraday and Darlene Ferrin, both those names contain, by morse code, the word "Easter." There is significant reason to believe he was picking his victims because of their names, because of the properties their names had. What I suspect happened is that they had multiple potential victims in each venue. Then, they simply chose the victim from those most appropriate or available at the time they wanted to commit the murder.

Q. Do you believe the Zodiac had more than the five or six victims that most people think?

A. Yes, I believe he had 11 victims in all. I believe, for example, Shelly Holmboe, a toddler in Los Gatos, who was abducted and murdered on October 19, 1969, Robert Salem in San Francisco on Stevenson Street which occurred March 29, 1970, Donna Lass, who was abducted from Lake Tahoe on September 6, 1970, Joan Webster, who was abducted and murdered in Boston on November 28, 1981, and Jane Scarlett, who was a collateral victim that died in a fire in

Riverside on June 18, 1981, which I say was set by the Zodiac.

Listen to the full interview with Ray on my website:

https://www.alanrwarren.com/hom-podcast-episodes/episode/92d8a6fa/zodiac-killer-solved-ray-grant-2015

---

1. Gareth Sewell Penn is an American true crime author and amateur detective known for being among the first non-journalists to write about the Zodiac Killer case. He published a theory about the killer's motives, publicly accused a noted UC Berkeley public policy professor of the crimes, and labeled himself a one-time suspect.

    Penn graduated from the University of California, Berkeley in 1962, with a Bachelor of Arts degree (B.A.) in Germanic languages and again in 1965 with a Master of Arts (MA) in Medieval Germanic languages. He received a Master of Library Science (MLS) from U.C. Berkeley in 1971.

    Penn says his father, Hugh Scott Penn, who had been a U.S. Army cryptographer during World War II, introduced him to the Zodiac case while he was working for the California Department of Justice.

Penn wrote two self-published books: *Times 17: The Amazing Story of the Zodiac Murders in California and Massachusetts, 1966-1981* released in 1987, and *The Second Power: A Mathematical Analysis of the letters attributed to the Zodiac murderer and supplement to Times 17* in 1999.

(https://en.wikipedia.org/wiki/Gareth_Penn)

2. Gareth Penn — Wikipedia. https://en.wikipedia.org/wiki/Gareth_Penn
3. Gareth Penn — Alchetron, The Free Social Encyclopedia. https://alchetron.com/Gareth-Penn

Zodiac Hoax

INTERVIEW WITH THOMAS HORAN

The fundamental premise of Thomas Horan's book, *The Myth of the Zodiac Killer: A Literary Investigation,* challenged the most basic, seemingly self-evident, assumption in any murder case. It questioned that the killer even existed.

This interview was our very first that covered the Zodiac Killer case, and he was saying that the Zodiac Killer never existed? We had to find out what this was all about.

We interviewed Horan three or four times, starting in 2014, primarily about the three books he had already written covering the Zodiac Hoax. At the time of the first interview, Horan had been involved in publishing for 25 years and was teaching reading and writing at the college level, from freshman Comp. to Textbook writing.

Q. What got you started on the Zodiac Killer case?

A. Well, like a lot of people, I do like to read true crime books, and especially the unsolved stuff like Jack the Ripper and the Zodiac Killer.

A few years ago, the original police department files from the case, the FBI files, became available to the public. Not officially, but they were leaked onto the internet. This was a unique opportunity to be able to read all of these documents for ourselves. Then we could draw our own conclusions about the murders and about the letters.

I was particularly interested because you have this person or character we think of as the Zodiac Killer, writing letters to the *San Francisco Chronicle* and a couple of other newspapers. Supposedly, that would give us a glimpse into the mind of this person and give us firsthand information about the killings. These letters were written in response to articles in the papers about the murders. So, it overlapped my field of expertise: reading and writing.

Q. In your opinion, what made the Zodiac murders unique?

A. It wasn't really unique. There was this very successful and very profitable story of the "Boston Strangler," a very similar situation. You had what looked like three separate serial killers strangling women in the Boston area. But they had distinctively different MOs. One of them turned out to be Albert DeSalvo, though he confessed to committing all of the murders. But there were pretty big holes in his confessions. With the last few victims, the younger, prettier victims, apparently, DeSalvo, a compulsive rapist, was copycatting this highly publicized Boston Strangler.

Part of the Boston Strangler myth was that the different police departments in the Boston area were not cooperating very effectively. So, you had a best-selling book by Gerald Frank, which is a pretty good work of true crime and investigative journalism, made into a highly fictionalized movie, starring Tony Curtis and Henry Fonda. Terribly fictionalized movie.

What's interesting is, when you read Graysmith's book on the Zodiac, you can tell he used the movie version of the Boston Strangler as his model of how he structured his book and how he presented his suspects and things. That movie was still playing in theatres. It was a blockbuster hit the night David and Betty-Lou were shot.

It's not really unique, and the media coverage borrows the tried and true elements of unsolved murder cases and questions why the police are having such a hard time finding this killer. But you throw into it the fact that the killer is actually writing letters to the newspapers. He got the audience involved in very clever ways. He demanded the papers publish these cryptograms, these coded messages on the front page of their paper. So, he got the audience involved in breaking these cryptograms-a pretty clever marketing idea in retrospect.

It worked. A couple of readers did solve it: a high school teacher and his wife solved the first ciphered message.

Q. There must have been a lot of pressure for the police to solve what looked like a serial killer, correct?

A. Well, one of the key investigators kind of got the ball rolling on this hysteria. His name was Mel Nicolai, and he was an agent with the California Department of Justice. He attended the seminar hosted by the FBI in getting the word out that you might have some unsolved murders in your area that don't look connected, but if double-checked, you might notice a same weapon, or same victim profile, or something.

He was really pushing this idea that these murders might be connected, kind of a power of suggestion, and he really seemed to have gotten carried away with the idea. Some of the investigators thought there might be a Zodiac Killer, but most were not convinced. But he did succeed in convincing some of the investigators that they were looking for a serial killer. With the Zodiac Killer, anybody could be a victim. And that sold a lot of newspapers.

Q. So, who was the cop's prime suspect, or did they have one?

A. At the time, they didn't have any. There were no serious suspects. The suspects that Graysmith talked about in his book were jokes as suspects. One police officer in Vallejo had investigated this fellow named Arthur Leigh Allen on charges of molesting children at the school where he worked. These are very credible allegations as he was later convicted of doing this kind of stuff.[1]

When the third attack happened, and the two kids were stabbed at Lake Berryessa, one of these pop culture psychologists diagnosed the Zodiac Killer as being a repressed latent homosexual and probably a child molester. This made a light go off in Sgt. Jack Mulanax's head because he knew about Allen's psychological problems. He also knew that Allen spent a lot of time at Lake Berryessa. He knew he lived with his mom, and he kind of fit the vague description they had of the assailant. It's reasonable, and you can see from Mulanax's point of view why he would think of Allen. He went around and even tried to convince people.

Most of the frame around Allen that Graysmith provided is complete bologna. It's interesting to read some of these documents that weren't published before and read them against Graysmith's claims in his books. Just exactly how far back did Graysmith start framing Allen? He claimed that he didn't even hear of Allen until 1980. But there were some indications of a third person who was actively trying to frame Allen for being the Zodiac way back in the early 70s.

So, other than Allen, and only a couple of people ever took Allen seriously as a suspect, they never really had a Zodiac suspect. It turns out there were very good suspects in most of these murders. In fact, the Benicia police department has always considered the first murder, the Faraday-Jensen murder, solved. Riverside police consider the Bates murder to be solved. I argued that the Vallejo police department pretty much solved the murder of Darlene Ferrin. There was a very good suspect, a very surprising suspect in the attack at Lake Berryessa, Cecelia Shepard died, and Bryan Hartnell lived. I see indications that San Francisco police sort of solved the Stine murder in 1997. They had a suspect in an unrelated murder that looked like a pretty good suspect for that shooting as well.

I'm not saying I can prove who committed each of these murders, but they're in the files. Graysmith never mentioned any of these suspects. There were solid suspects in each individual murder, but there was never a good suspect for all of the murders.

Q. Did they ever arrest anybody?

A. Well, there were arrests made, and some of the suspects were convicted of other murders. It's really expensive to put someone on trial for murder, especially when the mind of the public has been so confused. If you arrested somebody for any of these murders in these highly publicized cases, there's so much misinformation that it's almost impossible to get a reliable jury verdict in these cases. So they can convict these guys of other murders.

One of the top suspects in the Ferrin murder was even indicted in absentia for another drug-related murder, but he turned informant. He worked as an informant for a couple of years, but the cops in Vallejo he worked with were busted themselves for corruption. So, he eventually ended up going to prison on other drug charges in the late seventies.

There was one suspect the Riverside police were pretty sure murdered Cheri Jo Bates. They just never had quite enough evidence for an iron-clad case that would get a conviction. I'm not saying that these guys are definitely guilty. What I'm saying is there were good suspects in each of these murders, and none of them could be the Zodiac. The funny thing is Graysmith had access to most of this information and never said a word about them.[2]

Q. Were there any witnesses that survived being attacked by the Zodiac?

A. Well, a couple. Michael Mageau survived, but the poor guy is pretty messed up. He doesn't even remember how many times he was shot. Then Bryan Hartnell, the young man at Lake Berryessa, survived and recovered okay and became a lawyer. He doesn't talk to the media very often.

Q. So they never got a good description from those two surviving victims?

A. Well, Michael Mageau knew a lot more about who shot him than he admitted to the police. Darlene's family, her sister, and brother have also said, "Well, we weren't exactly honest with the police about what we were up to that night." That happens a lot, and it doesn't necessarily mean that Mike knows for sure. One suspect was booked in that shooting, but he didn't match the physical description. The gun that he had in his possession, a P38, which is the Walther version of a Lugar, was sent for comparison. There are still questions about if the ballistics matched. We just don't know what the results were. But he had a friend and part-time roommate who did match the description of the killer. The night he was arrested, he said that the gun wasn't his, and it belonged to somebody else. As soon as he was arrested, he knew he was going to be charged with murder.

Q. What can you tell us about the letters that came in from the Zodiac?

A. Well, the funny thing is that when those letters, if you have access to the files and the facts in these cases, started coming in and making claims like, "I was there, and I can tell you this, and I can tell you that." If you follow up on the claims in the letters, they point directly at the suspects and the fact that these suspects aren't being arrested.

Q. When did these letters start?

A. Well, on the night of July 4th, Mike and Darlene were shot in Blue Rock Springs Park, and there was a suspect arrested the night of July 20th. While he was being held, they found a P38, which is the type of weapon that was used in the shooting. They sent it off to the state crime lab for a ballistics check, but we don't know what the results were. The results came back around the 27th or 28th. By that time, Mike Mageau was shown a stack of mug photos of whatever suspects they had in this case, and he didn't recognize anybody.

A couple of days later, the three biggest newspapers in the Bay area, the *San Francisco Chronicle*, the *San Francisco*

Examiner, and the *Vallejo Times-Herald,* which were all owned by the same people, each received a letter. Each letter contained one-third of the famous 408-word cryptogram. There was a demand that the newspapers print this cryptogram on their front pages. The funny thing was that the letter writer didn't demand that the newspapers say why they were publishing these cryptograms. They did that on their own. The letter claimed that he was responsible for these two unsolved shootings, which the media already speculated that there was a connection.

They were characterized as "lovers' lane" shootings in the papers, but that's not really true. The spot where David and Betty-Lou were shot was not a lovers' lane by any stretch of the imagination. It was the parking lot of a water company pump house right along the highway between Benicia and Vallejo. There was no privacy in that lot at all. There was always at least one car going by every five minutes. These people could all see the kids sitting in their cars, so it was not a lovers' lane.

It was, however, known to be used by drug dealers, and the big-time traffickers would meet the little retail dealers in the parking lot. It was a difficult spot for the cops to patrol because you could see cars coming from either direction. You would get in a lot more trouble if you had five pounds of weed in your car, so they would break it up into smaller quantities, and the smaller retail dealers on into town. On the edge of Vallejo, there was Blue Rock Springs Park. And at that time, the parking lot was a lot darker and a little bit more remote. Some people used that parking lot as a lovers' lane. But on the night that Mike and Darlene were shot, you had cars going in and out of the lot, in and out, in and out, and not one of those was there on a date. But that is how the media portrayed it.

So, the letter took claim for the two shootings, and it said, "I will state certain facts in which only I and the police know." Well, if you follow up on those facts in the police reports, he gets some of the facts right, that's true. But some of them had already been published in the newspapers.

That kind of gives us a clue to which newspapers he was reading. Some of them were wrong. Some of his facts were just plain wrong, but apparently, he thought they were right. Some of the things he stated were actually facts that would not have been known by the killer. He especially referred to suspects in some of these letters that could not have been known to the killer. So, that was a really surprising thing that I discovered when I compared these letters and the actual police department files.

At the time, there were police officers like the Chief of Police in Vallejo, Jack Stilts, who did publicly say, "I don't believe this guy. We're not convinced by these letters." More or less, the media took the stand that these letters were confirmed by the facts in the cases. But they were not.

The nature of the cryptogram wouldn't hold up as evidence in court because of how he used multiple substitutions for different letters of the alphabet. For example, the cryptogram might actually say,

"I enjoy kissing people because it's so much fun." Not "killing." It could actually say "kissing" because man is the most dangerous animal of them all to kiss. I'm not sticking my entire reputation on that decoding, but it's possible that that's what it says.

The newspapers all subscribed to the theory these were from the killer, and there was no doubt about it. The police confirmed it. So, that was the impression that the public got.

Q. Do you think that someone who worked for the newspapers in San Francisco knew who was writing the letters?

A. There's no reliable story about how the newspapers responded when they opened these letters. It's clear that the letter writer demanded action by the end of the day, Friday, August 1st. But he didn't mail the letters until the afternoon of the 31st, and the morning papers would never have had time to respond to these letters.

So, did he know that? Is that also a clue that these letters were a hoax? Or was it just a mistake on his part? He seemed to know a lot about the newspaper business, and not just as a reporter, but as a publisher. For example, he never asked the newspapers to do anything illegal, which is odd. He never asked them to obstruct justice. It's like he knew what the procedures were.

Another interesting thing was, the *Vallejo Times-Herald* filed charges against this unknown person for attempted extortion. I mean, he's making threats of moral violence while he's demanding publicity on the front pages. The other newspapers didn't, but the *Vallejo Times* did, and the funny thing was he never wrote another letter to the *Vallejo Times-Herald*. How did he know they would file a complaint?

Q. So you think he was part of the newspaper somehow? Perhaps a reporter or editor?

A. The more letters that came in, the more newspaper articles were written, and the more police reports were written. Some of his facts were wrong, and some things that he thought were right were not right. You could trace them to very specific sources, very specific pages in certain police department reports.

Not only did the person writing the letters, but the person writing for the *Chronicle* had access to certain reports. By making a list of people who would have received these reports and had access to them at a certain window of time that the letters were written, you see a very short list of suspects. It came up with only two people- one person in Napa and one person in San Francisco. One of those two people happened to have handwriting identical to the handwriting on the Zodiac letters.

Q. Who were they?

A. There was a reporter at the *Chronicle*, and assuming his articles didn't have bylines, so assuming it was the same reporter, it was

Keith Power. That includes actual evidence tampering in the Stine case, where he not only picked up Stine's trip sheet but also would have had plenty of opportunities to grab a couple of pieces of his shirt and use them to write Zodiac letters.

The other person is a Napa Valley Deputy Sheriff, Hal Snook. He ran Napa's crime lab and happened to be on a very short list of people who were receiving copies of these police reports. There were rumors that these police forces were not working together even before the Zodiac case, but they were doing an excellent job and working together. There are also connections between him and some of the suspects. He would have known about these suspects in the two shootings not being fully investigated. So, he not only had access to the exact pages that the killer used to write the letters, but he would have known about these suspects not being investigated. I think that was his motive for participating in the hoax.

The same with Keith Power. I don't think it was a cheap publicity stunt, and I don't think it was a joke. I think they were actually trying to call attention to this problem without coming forward publicly, where their families would be in danger. I think that's how it started.

Q. So I guess there were no fingerprints on the letters?

A. There were plenty of fingerprints that undoubtedly belonged to people at the *Chronicle*, especially when they first started coming in as they didn't know. They got prank letters all the time, too, so the first letters probably had a lot of people's prints on them.

There were, in fact, fingerprints found on Darlene Ferrin's passenger car door handle. There were fingerprints found all over the passenger door of Brian's car in Lake Berryessa. There were a lot of fingerprints from a lot of crime scenes and a lot of fingerprints from Paul Stine's cab.

Now, there was a Napa Undersheriff, Tom Johnson, second in command of the Napa's Sheriff Department, who was not really well trained, but he had been there for a long time. He had a press conference where he announced that preliminary analysis appeared to match some of these fingerprints from all three crime scenes, and possibly to one of the letters.

A couple of days later, when they got the actual reports back from the FBI, it said no, there was no match between these prints. So, why did Johnson say that? The only person who could have told him there was a match was Hal Snook. Snook would have been the only person in a position to tell Tom Johnson they had found a match between all of these prints.

Q. What are your thoughts on if the letters came from more than one person?

A. The handwriting is very distinctive in some funny ways. It depends on which copies you look at. A lot of the handwriting experts at the time who were spouting off

ZODIAC HOAX

opinions were not looking at the original letters. They were looking at plain old xerox copies.

There are a lot of details about the strokes used because all the letters were written with a blue felt tip pen. That interested me because, in my previous experience with forgers, your first clue that a signature is a forgery is that they use a blue felt tip pen. They don't have a lot of confidence in their strokes.

In the process of looking for fingerprints, they sprayed these letters with a solution called ninhydrin, which chemically cause the fingerprints to show up. But it caused the ink to run, and that's interesting because you can get a lot of information about where he starts his stroke, and where he stops his stroke, or if he hesitates or lifts the pen.

In looking at the first three letters that people have made a high-resolution color scan of, you can see this information. It looked to me as though the person writing the Zodiac letters had done a few things to disguise his handprint. One was to rotate the paper about 90-degrees counterclockwise to create an exaggerated rightward slant in his handwriting. The second thing was to rotate the paper 180-degrees and draw certain letters upside down-the lowercase B, D, P, G, Y, and lowercase H. You can see this in the strokes.

Maybe I'm right about that, or maybe I'm wrong. But after the Stine shooting, we started getting letters that seemed like the personality changed, and the purpose of writing the letters changed. You notice those strokes are reversed. Whoever's writing those letters started by rotating the paper and started writing certain letters of the alphabet, and then they stopped doing it. Maybe it was the same person that stopped doing it, but that's a pretty big clue.

In addition to the personality changes, he's no longer making any credible claims about any connection to any of the murders. He's not sticking his nose into any real murder investigations. These are long and rambling letters like the one he wrote to Melvin Belli.[3] There were a lot of clues that whoever wrote the first three or four letters stopped. There was a reason, and we can see why he probably stopped. Then you see somebody else took over writing the letters.

Q. Why did someone else take over writing the letters? Were they an accomplice? Or was it someone else who was looking for fame?

A. Well, this was a huge story for the *Chronicle,* and it appeared that after the cab driver was shot in October of '69, there was a big conference of all the different law enforcement agencies on October 20th. That's when you see the handwriting change, and it looks like a completely different person took over writing the letters.

I don't think it was a coincidence, because Hal Snook would have been one of the participants at this conference. After the conference, literally a couple of days, Keith Power never wrote another article about the Zodiac ever again, and Paul Avery[4] took over as Zodiac's publicist. Paul Avery was not the original reporter on the Zodiac story. He actually wrote a couple of stories questioning the credibility of the Zodiac letters.

So, something changed after that law enforcement conference in October. The *Chronicle* wanted to keep those letters coming. There were two people who were pretty strong suspects for doing that. One was Paul Avery, and it turned out for a lot of reasons, the other being Robert Graysmith, the person who just kept writing Zodiac letters.

Q. What about the reporters of the *Chronicle* having access to the police reports?

A. There was a *Chronicle* reporter who undoubtedly had access. For example, Richard Hoffman, the undercover narcotics officer in his own report, put himself at the scene of a crime at the time of the shooting. It may have been part of the reason there was a shooting. He was the only Vallejo officer to type his report the night of the shooting. In the early morning hours of July 5th, he typed his report and went home.

That day, a *Chronicle* reporter got a copy of that report, either physically, or it was read to him over the phone because he wrote an article. His article was based exclusively and extensively on Hoffman's report. Interestingly, those first two Zodiac letters, he seemed to also have had a copy of that because he was correcting the one or two things the *Chronicle* reporter not only got wrong but imitated 17 unique spelling errors that Hoffman made in his report.

It's pretty compelling that both the *Chronicle* reporter's and the so-called Zodiac Killer's source of information that week happened to be Hoffman's report. Were they trying to frame Hoffman? Hoffman said a few things over the years that tended to make him look guilty. I just think that if he were guilty of participating in the shooting, he would have done a much better job covering his tracks. He was the one who rode with the victims in the ambulance. A lot of people have suspected him of being involved in the shooting, but I'm not so sure of that. There's no doubt whatsoever that a *Chronicle* reporter and the guy writing the Zodiac letter both had a copy of Hoffman's report.

Q. Robert Graysmith wrote a couple of Zodiac books, yet you tie him to the Zodiac murders.

A. What's really weird is that in Graysmith's book, *Zodiac,* every cop that sneezed on a piece of paper related to the Zodiac case got his name in Graysmith's book. Even the guy at the San Francisco Coroner's office where they had the evidence room, the guy who signed in the evidence on the Stine case, George Schultz, his name was in Graysmith's book. All he did was just sign for the evidence and turned it into the evidence locker. His name is in Graysmith's book.

There are two names absent from Graysmith's book-Hal Snook and Keith Power. In fact, Graysmith actually lied about who was writing which newspaper articles. He also plagiarized quite a bit. He claimed to have interviewed a witness, and it's actually that section of the book that's plagiarized from a newspaper article. But he just flat out lied about who was writing what stories at the time. Keith Power was coming up with the stuff. So, that's another pretty big clue. Why would Graysmith leave their names out of his book? Especially when it turns out that he and Hal Snook go back a really long time. Apparently, they went way back.

Q. Anything else on Graysmith?

A. He's an interesting character, and not totally honest either. First of all, he changed his name. The first time he tried to publish a book about Zodiac, he changed his name. His actual name was Robert Smith Jr. His dad was a Colonel in the Airforce. He spent quite a few years in Japan. When he was 12-years old, he got his first job writing for a newspaper, the *Stars and Stripes Network*, as an illustrator and working in the darkroom. Where did he get the skills to get a job like that at 12? He worked for newspapers all his life. He worked for the *Oakland Tribune* for four years while he got his degree. Then, he went to work for the *Chronicle*.

He wasn't just an illustrator; he worked in the darkroom. Newspapers call their production department the darkroom. So, when the letters started coming into the *Chronicle*, Graysmith was the one photographing them. They always came in when he was working. They never came into the *Chronicle* on Graysmith's day off, and all the letters were mailed on his days off.

In his book, there was this question on how Zodiac disguised his handwriting, and Graysmith came up with this explanation for how you can copy Zodiac handwriting. If you look at the letters themselves, when he wrote his book, there were no photocopies of the letters available. You can see it's not what Zodiac did. He didn't trace the letters from a master alphabet. He actually put the letters on top of each other. Especially the first few letters, that's not how it was done. But it is how he (Graysmith) could have done it.

There are lots and lots of clues that point towards Graysmith, at least writing the Belli Letter. He made a lot of claims about the Belli Letter that he cut out of his book, things like that. He himself is pretty suspicious, and he's told so many lies over the years. His frame around Arthur Leigh Allen is such a pile of crap. He's already been exposed for that. All his other true crime books have been thoroughly debunked. He tells lies about the authenticity of the letters, and why would he do that unless they were a hoax.

Q. When did Graysmith get into this?

A. If you watch the movie and the story of how Graysmith got into it, it's obvious that it was not true. He had been involved much longer than he claimed. My only question is just exactly when did he start? Was he in on it from the very beginning? Or did he just steal the idea and run off with it?

Q. So, is there anything that ties these murders together?

A. There's no evidence of any kind that ties these murders together. Not a weapon, not a MO. The MOs are quite a bit different.

The guy who did the shooting on Lake Herman Road obviously killed people before. The shooting at Blue Rock Springs Park was a lot sloppier. A different weapon was used every time. The media reported that the same weapon was used to shoot Paul Stine that had been used at the Blue Rock Springs Park, but it was a completely different type of 9 mm pistol. The witness descriptions were actually quite different. Graysmith kind of fudges them and sometimes just flat out lied about them to make it sound like they're describing the same guy, but they were not.

The famous "Fouke Memo" described a suspect who couldn't possibly be the guy who shot Stine. He was 50-60 pounds heavier, a couple of inches taller, and 20-years older. He had blonde hair instead of brown hair. So, it couldn't possibly be the same guy. Graysmith made it sound like the descriptions matched, and they didn't.

Officer Fouke Memo

Listen to the full interviews with Thomas on my website:

https://www.alanrwarren.com/hom-podcast-episodes/episode/88859ea7/zodiac-killer-myth-pt-1-thomas-horan-2014

https://www.alanrwarren.com/hom-podcast-episodes/episode/955854a6/zodiac-killer-myth-pt-2-thomas-horan-2014

https://www.alanrwarren.com/hom-podcast-episodes/episode/7aa87ec5/zodiac-revisited-thomas-horan-2015

1. Arthur Leigh Allen was the prime suspect of law enforcement in the case for the Zodiac Killer. Allen became publicly known as a Zodiac suspect shortly after the release of *Zodiac*, a book authored by Robert Graysmith. Allen was cleared through a comparison of DNA, fingerprints, palm prints, and handwriting. In 1991, surviving victim, Mike Mageau, picked Allen out of a police lineup. Surviving victim, Bryan Hartnell, identified his voice and physical appearance as being similar to the Zodiac. Arthur Leigh Allen died on August 26, 1992, at the age of 58 of a heart attack in his home in Vallejo. (Arthur Leigh Allen | Zodiac Killer Wiki | Fandom. https://zodiackiller.fandom.com/wiki/Arthur_Leigh_Allen)

2. Robert Graysmith worked as a political cartoonist for the *San Francisco Chronicle* in 1969 when the Zodiac Killer case came to prominence. He attempted to decode letters written by the killer and became obsessed with the case over the next 13 years. Graysmith wrote two books about the case. His 1986 book, *Zodiac,* was the basis for the 2007 film by the same name. He eventually gave up his career as a cartoonist to write five more books on high-profile

crimes. (Robert Graysmith — Wikipedia. https://en.wikipedia.org/wiki/Robert_Graysmith)

3. Melvin Belli was a prominent American lawyer. He had many celebrity clients, including Zsa Zsa Gabor, Errol Flynn, Chuck Berry, Muhammad Ali, The Rolling Stones, Jim Bakker and Tammy Faye Bakker, Martha Mitchell, Maureen Connolly, Lana Turner, Tony Curtis, and Mae West. During his legal career, he won over $600 million in damages for his clients. He was also the attorney for Jack Ruby, who shot Lee Harvey Oswald for the assassination of President John F. Kennedy. (https://wikimili.com/en/Melvin_Belli)

4. Paul Avery was an American journalist, best known for his reporting on the serial killer known as the Zodiac, and later for his work on the Patricia Hearst kidnapping. Avery reported on the Zodiac case, a series of killings—unsolved to this day—that began in December 1968 and ostensibly ended with the death of a San Francisco cab driver in October 1969. At the time, Avery was a police reporter for the *San Francisco Chronicle*. For a long time, it was thought that the Zodiac's activities were limited to the Bay Area, but Avery discovered a 1966 murder in Riverside that he linked to the Zodiac. The Zodiac soon wrote Avery misspelled by the Zodiac as "Averly," a Halloween card, warning, "You are doomed." The front of the card read, "From your secret pal: I feel it in my bones/you ache to know my name/and so I'll clue you in…" Then inside: "But why spoil the game?" Just as quickly as the threat was made public, a fellow journalist made up hundreds of campaign-style buttons, worn by nearly everyone on the *Chronicle* staff, including Avery, that said, "I Am Not Paul Avery." It was at this time that Avery began carrying a .38 caliber revolver. (Paul Avery — Alchetron, The Free Social Encyclopedia. https://alchetron.com/Paul-Avery)

The Zodiac 340 Cipher: Mystery Solved

BY MICHAEL BUTTERFIELD

Over the years, I have heard many rumors about some break in the case and proposed solutions to the Zodiac's unsolved ciphers. Every amateur codebreaker is certain that their solution is correct, but the evidence debunks their claims. The result is immediate skepticism whenever someone declares that they have unlocked the secrets of a Zodiac cipher. One learns not to get too excited about such claims in order to avoid the inevitable disappointment.

Several years ago, I came to rely on David Oranchak for guidance when trying to understand the many complex issues surrounding the

Zodiac's ciphers. A computer programmer, David's approach to the ciphers was refreshing, and his analysis was informative. I often receive emails from people who claim to have solved the ciphers, and I always refer them to David for his examination and conclusions. He continually provides a fair assessment of proposed solutions and encourages people to bring new ideas to the discussion. His website *ZodiacKillerCiphers.com* has been a valuable resource for anyone seeking information about the ciphers.

For these and other reasons, I was not immediately skeptical when I received a message from David on the morning of Saturday, December 5th, which read: "I and two other programmers have a solution for the 340 Cipher. No joke. I just sent off the solve to the FBI. I'm pretty sure it's correct."

I believed that David would not make such claims if he could not back them up with clear evidence, so I was instantly intrigued by the thought that such evidence was forthcoming, and I was not disappointed. I soon learned the incredible story behind the solution, a story about pursuing a

THE ZODIAC 340 CIPHER: MYSTERY SOLVED

seemingly random clue in a mundane search of data.

The collaborative efforts of three individuals in different countries across the globe finally solved the mystery. From his home in Flanders, Belgium, computer programmer Jarl Van Eycke worked online with David Oranchak in the United States, and Sam Blake in Melbourne, Australia.

As members of Mike Morford's forum at *ZodiacKillerSite.com*, the trio shared information, examined possible decryption methods, and searched for any clue which could crack the Zodiac's three unsolved ciphers. Van Eycke created "AZdecrypt," described by David as "a fast and powerful cipher solver," and a modified version of this software helped Van Eycke and entrepreneur Louie Helm set a world record for the deciphering of a bigram substitution of the shortest cipher length.

Studying the Zodiac's 340 Cipher, Sam identified and collected information about variations in the ciphertext, which ultimately proved to be the key to cracking the cipher. "My main contribution here was actually enumerating many possible reading directions through the cipher, in total over 650,000," Sam explained. "David and I both ran these through AZdecrypt and ZKdecrypto, respectively. Interestingly, only AZdecrypt was able to find the fragments of the complete solution. It was a needle in a haystack. Even finding the right haystack to search in was lucky."

"Just one very partial solution, in a sea of 650,000 cipher variations I was running," David added. That one partial solution was not entirely correct but instead suggested information about the cipher's construction. "By luck, we discovered that (Zodiac) split it into three pieces and rearranged the message in a predictable diagonal pattern in the first two pieces." When the words ended at the right side of the text block, the diagonal message would continue in the next line on the left side. The Zodiac made an apparent effort to thwart attempts to decipher the message by constructing the cipher in this way. The resulting block of text may have been intended to encourage the false assumption that the 340 Cipher was created using the same methods as the killer's previous cipher, a simple message reading from left to right as regular text. By rearranging the message into three parts

THE ZODIAC 340 CIPHER: MYSTERY SOLVED 209

disguised as one block of text, the Zodiac may have believed that most people would never look beyond its appearance to discover the actual method used to hide the real message.

David explained, "Cracking it required undoing those arrangements then trying to discover his substitution key. That wasn't enough because he made some mistakes in the second piece. Jarl discovered the mistakes and corrected them, which greatly cleared up the second piece." After Jarl's corrections were included and the proper adjustments made, the decryption process quickly produced actual results. "We had a nugget of a solution on Thursday. I took Friday off and worked on it all day. My teammates Sam and Jarl also worked on it a lot. By (Saturday) morning, Jarl had worked out the remaining bit, and it was finally complete enough to send off to the FBI. They responded almost immediately." David said that he had received three telephone calls from the Bureau on Saturday morning. "When I talked to the FBI, they only needed to make one change to the solution." David and his team had deciphered a section of six letters to read, "soo her." "We couldn't figure out the part that says, 'soo her,' [but] their cryptanalyst called me, and she said she thinks it's supposed to say, "sooner" instead."

Dan Olson, Cryptanalyst Forensic Examiner for the FBI's Racketeering Records Analysis Unit in Washington, D.C., also examined the solution. Oranchak said, "They are running the solution up the chain now. Dan says it looks solid. I was happy to hear Dan Olson tell me personally that he thinks it's solid."

During his appearance in the 2009 History Channel series *MysteryQuest*, Dan Olson shared his theory that the text block of the Z340 may have been intended to be separated into two parts to be deciphered. Actually, the cipher was split into three parts, and the message was found in the first two parts.

The FBI experts were so confident that the solution was valid that the Bureau essentially closed the file on the 340 Cipher. "FBI is amending their original report to include our solution as the actual solution," David reported, "Then they'll submit it back to the San Francisco Police Department (the original requestor of assistance with the cipher in 1969)."

THE ZODIAC 340 CIPHER: MYSTERY SOLVED

The solution revealed a message that seemed consistent with the Zodiac's persona and character as displayed in his previous communications, including the 408 symbol cipher's deciphered text. In that message, the killer wrote that he was killing people to collect slaves to serve him during his afterlife in "paradice." The Zodiac also included the same misspelling in the text, using the words "paradice" and "slaves" to form a cross. In the solution to the 340, the writer returned to this theme and declared that he was not afraid of death.

> *I HOPE YOU ARE HAVING LOTS OF FUN IN TRYING TO CATCH ME THAT WASN'T ME ON THE TV SHOW WHICH BRINGS UP A POINT ABOUT ME I AM NOT AFRAID OF THE GAS CHAMBER BECAUSE IT WILL SEND ME TO PARADICE ALL THE SOONER BECAUSE I NOW HAVE ENOUGH SLAVES TO WORK FOR ME WHERE EVERYONE ELSE HAS NOTHING WHEN THEY REACH PARADICE SO THEY ARE AFRAID OF DEATH I AM NOT AFRAID BECAUSE I KNOW THAT MY NEW LIFE WILL BE AN EASY ONE IN PARADICE DEATH*

David noted that, unlike other proposed solutions, this new solution revealed a clear and discernible message. "(We) didn't have to do too many steps, and yet a coherent message pops out."

The writer referred to the Bay Area television talk show, *The Jim Dunbar Show,* and an episode featuring famous attorney Melvin Belli. On October 22, 1969, someone called the Oakland police station and claimed to the Zodiac. The caller demanded that Belli, or Boston attorney F. Lee Bailey, appear on the show with host Jim Dunbar.

During the broadcast, a man called several times but kept hanging up to prevent police from tracing the calls to his location. The caller agreed to be referred to as "Sam" and complained that headaches had driven him to murderous impulses. "Sam" expressed his fears of being "hurt," and Belli promised to help the caller avoid "the gas chamber." After the broadcast, a recording of the caller's voice was played for the three people who had spoken to the Zodiac. Surviving victim Bryan Hartnell and police dispatchers David Slaight and Nancy Slover all confirmed that "Sam" was not the Zodiac. Police reports, FBI files, and other accounts indicated that "Sam" later called Melvin Belli's home several times and that police were finally able to trace those calls to a patient in a mental institution. Investigators concluded that the man was not the Zodiac. Still, the incident became an often misunderstood chapter of the story, and some people continued to believe that "Sam" was the killer.

The writer of the ciphertext stated, "That wasn't me on the TV show." The incident with Sam occurred on October 22, 1969, and Zodiac's cipher was sent two and a half weeks later in November. On December 20, 1969, the Zodiac sent a letter to Belli's home in an envelope containing a piece of a victim's bloodstained shirt to confirm the writer's identity as the real killer. The tone and text of the letter's message seemed somewhat insincere, and the message could be interpreted as a mockery of Sam's imposter version of the "Zodiac" character.

At first, David said that he did not expect much to come from the possible decipher method, but everything changed when a message materialized before his eyes. "When the words 'that wasn't me on the TV show' popped out during the solve, I jumped out of my chair and said, 'Holy ****!' since that show happened like a few weeks before the cipher was received. That's when I knew it was on the right track."

Thanks to the extraordinary efforts of three men working together from different parts of the world, the mystery of the 340 Cipher had finally been solved after more than fifty years. "It's exciting. We were really lucky to come across this solution," David said. "It was only a handful of words to start with. Could have very easily ignored them and moved on. But 'gas chamber' really stood out."

When David explained how the cipher was solved, I was reminded of his previous statements in interviews for my podcast series about possible decryption methods and different theories about the construction of the ciphers. I said to him, "This really bolsters so many things you said in your interviews." David replied, "Yeah, the statistics in the ciphertext really did turn out to reflect the way it was constructed.'

In November 2019, David and I were discussing the Zodiac's 340 Cipher for the podcast *ZODIAC: A TO Z*, "Ep. #8 – 340: The Mystery." Approximately 15 minutes into the show, David essentially predicted how the Z340 was constructed when he described possible encryption techniques. "Route transpositions are things like, read the message from left to right and then right to left and then left to right, kind of like a snake pattern, back and forth, a zigzag pattern. That's an example of a route transposition. Or like, a diagonal, reading off the message diagonally. So in those situations, you'd end up with a plain text that doesn't look like it makes any sense. And then, the last step would be to encrypt it using the same kind of substitution used in the first cipher. So the symbols are assigned to each of the letters."

For years, I stated my belief that the Zodiac may have been somewhat disappointed his first cipher was solved so quickly and, therefore, he may have intended the next cipher to be more challenging to solve. Some people speculated that amateur codebreakers Donald and Betty Harden were able to solve the original 408 Cipher so quickly because the Zodiac was little more than an amateur who possessed only a basic understanding of cryptography. I asked David if this new cipher solution cast doubt on those theories about the Zodiac's cryptography knowledge. "Yes, either he knew codes or had a good intuition about how to make them." David also agreed with my theory. "He definitely reacted to the Hardens solution and made it much harder."

David thanked Mike Morford, owner of *ZodiacKillerSite.com*, and stated, "the site played a crucial role" in the events leading up to the solution. "It gave us a forum to collaborate. Me and the other nerds used it extensively. This could have only happened with the two other guys I worked with. Sam (Blake) sent me the 650,000 variations. One of them turned out to be extremely close to the right answer. And Jarl built the codebreaking software and also helped fix up the solution. No way I could have done any of this without them." Jarl Van Eycke said, "It is unbelievable how everything came together so perfectly between the three of us. And I am so happy to be a part of it."

David was concerned that media coverage about the solution could be confusing. "It may be hard to convey to the general public because it does require additional steps — diagonal reading, splitting into three sections, fixing the mistakes, and rearranging letters in the last two lines." He has produced a new episode of his YouTube video series *Let's Crack Zodiac*, "Ep. #5 - The 340 Is Solved" with more details about the new solution and the methods used to decipher the message.

While the new solution did not provide any apparent clues to the killer's identity, the deciphered message revealed another glimpse into the mind of the Zodiac. Whether or not he believed his dead victims would serve as his slaves in his afterlife, the repeated theme was somehow important to the killer. In 1969, the Zodiac claimed he was killing victims to become his slaves, and, more than half a century later, the theme remains significant because those victims were sacrificed to achieve his infamy. As his story continues to unfold in the pages of the history books, we are still haunted by the ghost of the Zodiac.

FBI Statement:

The FBI has a team of cryptanalysis experts that decipher coded messages, symbols, and records from criminals known as the Cryptanalysis and Racketeering Records Unit. CRRU regularly works with the cryptologic research community to solve ciphers. On December 5, 2020, the FBI received the solution to a cipher popularly known as Z340 from a cryptologic researcher and independently verified the decryption. Cipher Z340 is one of four ciphers attributed to the Zodiac Killer. This cipher was first submitted to the FBI Laboratory on November 13, 1969, but not successfully decrypted. Over the past 51 years, CRRU has reviewed numerous proposed solutions from the public – none of which had merit. The cipher was recently solved by a team of three private citizens. The Zodiac Killer case remains an ongoing investigation for the FBI San Francisco Division and our local law enforcement partners. The Zodiac Killer terrorized multiple communities across Northern California, and even though decades have gone by, we continue to seek justice for the victims of these brutal crimes. Due to the ongoing nature of the investigation and out of respect for the victims and their families, we will not be providing further comment at this time.

References

All interviews were taken from the the *House of Mystery Radio Show* between 2010 and 2020. The show airs on several radio stations throughout the United States, including

- KKNW 1150 A.M. in Seattle/Tacoma,
- KCAA 106.5 F.M. in Los Angeles,
- KCAA 102.3 F.M. Riverside,
- KCAA 1050 A.M. Palm Springs,
- KFNX 1100 A.M. Phoenix,
- KFNX 540 A.M. Salt Lake City,
- on my website: *alanrwarren.com/house-of-mystery-radioshow*

Below is a list of our guests and their works in reference to the Zodiac Killer:

1. Beeson, Drew: *Sighting In On The Zodiac Killer: Unmasking America's Most Puzzling Unsolved Murders*, December 24, 2019, ISBN: 978-1679201974.
2. Penn, Anne: *What if? Golden State Killer —*

Zodiac Solved, September 25, 2019, ISBN: 978-1693971747.
3. Morford, Mike: *The Case of the Zodiac Killer: The Complete Transcript with Additional Commentary, Photographs and Documents,* WildBlue Press, May 24, 2018, ISBN: 978-1947290532.
4. Oranchak, David: Zodiac Ciphers,
5. Hewitt, Mark: *Zodiac Killer Revealed,* Genius Book Publishing, September 25, 2018, ISBN: 978-1947521032.
6. Stewart, Gary L.: *The Most Dangerous Animal of All: Searching for my Father and Finding the Zodiac Killer,* Harper Paperbacks, May 12, 2015, ISBN: 978-0062313171.
7. Hodel, Steve: *Most Evil: Avenger, Zodiac, and the Further Serial Murders of Dr. George Hill Hodel,* Berkley Books, September 7, 2010, ISBN: 978-0425236314.
8. Grant, Ray: *Zodiac Killer Solved: a detailed solution to the most infamous serial murder case of the 20th century,* October 20, 2020, ASIN: B08LLBBC4N.
9. Horan, Thomas Henry: *The Myth of the Zodiac Killer: A Literary Investigation,*

January 21, 2020, ISBN: 979-8601798327.
10. Sty, Jim: *Zodiac Killer Discussion Facebook Group*
11. Butterfield, Michael: *zodiackillerfacts.com*
12. Morford, Mike: *zodiackillersite.com*
13. Oranchak, David: *zodiackillerciphers.com*

About Alan R. Warren

Alan R. Warren has written several bestselling True Crime books and has been one of the hosts and producers of the popular NBC news talk radio show the *House of Mystery,* which reviews True Crime, History, Science, Religion, Paranormal mysteries that we live with every day. From a darker, comedic, and logical perspective, he has interviewed guests such as Robert Kennedy Jr., F. Lee Bailey, Aphrodite Jones, Marcia Clark, Nancy Grace, Dan Abrams, and Jesse Ventura. The show is based in Seattle on KKNW 1150 AM and syndicated on the NBC network throughout the United States, including on KCAA 106.5 FM Los

Angeles/Riverside/Palm Springs, as well in Utah, New Mexico, and Arizona.

Read more about Alan on his website:
www.alanrwarren.com

About Michael Butterfield

Michael Butterfield (*zodiackillerfacts.com*) is a writer who has conducted extensive research on the Zodiac case since the 1990s. As a recognized leading expert on the unsolved crime, he has served as a media source and consultant for news articles, documentaries, the History Channel series *The Hunt for the Zodiac Killer*, and Director David Fincher's major motion picture *Zodiac*. Butterfield has also consulted on the following: the Zodiac documentary *Case Reopened*, the History Channel series *Mystery Quest*, the E! Canada series *The Shocking Truth*, the Reelz Channel documentary *The Real Story of Zodiac*, the HLN series *Very Scary People*, the documentary produced for Japanese television *Darkside Mystery*, and the podcast series *Monster: The Zodiac Killer*. He is also the producer of the podcast series *Zodiac: A to Z*. He is a contributing author for *True Crime: Case Files*, *True Crime Magazine*, and the two-volume collection of essays titled *A History of Evil in Pop Culture*.

Read more about Michael on his website: zolicakillerfacts.com

Also in the House of Mystery Radio Show Interview Series

The *House of Mystery Radio Show* has been on the air for ten years, broadcasting in over a dozen cities in the U.S. It started as a way to interview guests knowledgeable in many of the world's mysteries involving crime, science, religion, history, paranormal, conspiracies, etc. The House of Mystery Interview series is a curated collection of interviews from the show. Each volume focuses on one of the mysteries, providing the background and reproducing the main points discussed in the interviews. There will be no committed answer at the end, as the Interviews series does not attempt to solve the case. Instead, it provides the most compelling aspects of each theory held by different experts. This series is an excellent reference for researchers and a good overview for those unfamiliar with the case. Online links to the actual interviews are included.

VOLUME 1: JACK THE RIPPER: THE INTERVIEWS

Volume 1 of the Interview Series, "Jack the Ripper," covers the ultimate "who-done-it" mystery of 1888 London. Scotland Yard's "Whitechapel Murder File," in which Jack the Ripper had a starring role, went cold before it could be solved. One hundred thirty-two years later, and the fascination with this cold case mystery continues. Ripperologists passionately debate suspects, opinions, research methods, and theories. Even which murder victims to include in the case is widely debated. Astonishingly, work continues, and today Ripperologists still find new clues that bring us closer to solving the mystery.

The mix of credible and diverse thinkers interviewed includes world-renowned historian Neil Storey, the Godfather of Ripper Research, Paul Begg, Ripperologists: Paul Williams, Tom Wescott, Adam Wood, and Steve Blomer. Michael Hawley contributes his unprecedented scientific approach to the case. Suspect Ripperologists Jeff Mudgett, whose great-great-grandfather was serial killer H.H. Holmes, weighs in, as does Russell Edwards, who believes he solved the mystery through DNA.

VOLUME 2: JFK ASSASSINATION: THE INTERVIEWS

Volume 2 of the Interview Series, "JFK Assassination," covers *the* unrivaled historical mystery of historical mysteries. The JFK assassination is the grandfather of all conspiracies in America and arguably where they all started. A highly popular President with movie star looks and charisma, effecting significant changes in society, was brutally cut down in his prime. The official story was that JFK was killed by a sole assassin, Lee Harvey Oswald. However, many conspiracy theorists believe in an assassination plot involving the FBI, CIA, U.S. military, VP LBJ, Cuba's Fidel Castro, Russia's KGB, the Mafia, or some combination of those entities.

The research and interviewing of the JFK assassination experts lasted for over six years. Arguments and counter-arguments from a diverse mix of bestselling authors make for some interesting discussions. And some of the authors interviewed are considered just as controversial as the mystery itself. Most authors focused on who they believe was responsible for the assassination. Others narrowed their focus on certain related aspects, such as the Zapruder film, Nix film, Garrison Tapes, etc. All information collected from each expert adds value to the overall mystery.

www.ingramcontent.com/pod-product-compliance
Lightning Source LLC
Chambersburg PA
CBHW071428070526
44578CB00001B/27